Twin Love

Divine Counterpart

Sarah Ince

On the long spiral home to the creator,

We are to meet our Twin Love,

True love reunited…

Our divine compliment (divine counterpart),

The sacred reunion.

Manifesting the highest love

A love so true, haunts our heart
Awaiting for the moment of fulfilment
Of that sacred union, oh so true
The heart quivers in anticipation
Of the realisation of a love so true
The soul is ever seeking this special ONE
That knows you more than you know yourself
Swift relief is upon the moment of reunion
Love cascading, a divine marriage of Love
It is with this vision these works are birthed
That the meeting and reunions of a love so pure
Begin and are assisted in finding the ONE

Dedication

It is to you, my divine beloved, that I dedicate this edition to, to our physical meeting, to our merger, our sacred union. As we share the sacred soul remembrance that our two life essences originally were one~ as we now share our lives in sacred celebration of our eternal love. As above, so below, let our love flow to one another~

Innocent

Innocent I am
Pure spirit
Pure radiance
Clear of all imprints
Now – no past
Reborn anew

Contents

Love = Unity, Unity = Love

Foreword

Many of us have searched many lifetimes to find the true one of our hearts to rejoin with – to journey back "home" to the oneness with. Twin Love material originated from a series of taught workshops from 2003 to 2009. The first workshop, Twin Flame, took place in Maldon, Essex on Valentine's Day 2003. The poetry section of this book formed the vibrational connection to energetically anchoring this connection for each participant. Later the same year, Twin Ray workshop was released in Glastonbury, also with the material in the poetry section of this book. Both of these first workshops propelled each participant on their path to their beloved. The third workshop, Twin Essence, was anchored in Suffolk. The Fourth workshop, Twin Spirit, was anchored on the island of Cyprus, amidst luscious surroundings that truly upheld the energies of Aphrodite. The sites of Aphrodite were visited, and a very high energy surrounded the entire workshop. The Fifth Workshop took place in the UK. The most recent channelling took place in France: - Quintessence of Love and Divine Love Realised. Divine Love Realised was originally channelled mid year of 2008, although the essential sacred site anchorage took place in April 2009 at the exotic garden in Monaco. Quintessence of Love is officially the last "level" of this book, but the meditation in Monaco somehow seems to crown these works. The meditation included is a transcript of the recording, which is available as an MP3 download (online – internet).

Each chapter builds upon the other, offering a deep heart opening that attracts to you new levels of love – that of a soul nature. The formats vary from written meditation instruction, insights, and practical exercises – to sacred coded artwork – to sacred poetry and invocations – all offering a multi-level, multi-faceted, multi-layered building of the sacred twin energies. All the information is from the highest sacred levels.

The book is best read in a peaceful environment where you may feel the energies as you connect to this book, and allow the shifts that your soul is calling you to.

At the time of the most recent book release, my vibration is held high to meet my own dear life partner – in the flesh, for the realisation of the highest vision of love flames ever known to walk the sacred path of physical life – hand in hand, heart to heart, as ONE.I bless you also to find you're ONE.

This new edition that you now hold in your hands, includes new love poetry, which resonates with new learning of the love paradigms. We must be whole within at this time to be on the vibrational resonance of our own truth – in order to meet our beloved. This involves a moving away from all karmic relationships based on anything less than unconditional love.

Thoughts to turn you inward – to the source of your life
On Doubt

Doubt can turn the object of your doubting, to match the thoughts of doubt: - but this does not mean that "you were right", but rather under the law of free will and your ability to influence your own world, you are able to discredit the credible: - you may see it anyway you want to see it: - the universe obliges. If you want to be a doubter – then you are free to cast those thoughts of disbelief on all manner of glory, at which point it is "cast out" of your life: - because you said "It does not exist". Then it will swiftly move out of your sphere only, and onto elsewhere, where those are ready to receive it.

Chapter 1

Twin Essence

Entering the original twin of love, the other half of your soul
Known as your twin essence

Sweetness arise in me
To reflect the flame of twin love
As above, so below
From him to me
~Eternally~
Love is the greatest healing power of all, with the great ability to transform

The divine love connection teachings
Brought to you from the divine temples of love
To your own inner divine temple: - In your heart

One in Essence: - We return

The Twin Essence relationship is the core main connection, the other half of our soul. Once this is healed, whether it is possible to be together or not in this lifetime, all doors open to heal all wounds that you may go from bud to flower.

To one degree or another, with soul relationships, if you feel pain, so does the other. In Twin Essence coupling, this is magnified, as you ARE one another, it is literally impossible not to feel to some degree.

Expressions you thought were hidden parts of yourself turn out to be your Twin Essence. Once you have met your twin essence, a lot in your life that may have mystified you, suddenly becomes clear.

Twin Essence

Ancient rings of promise
Brought before us once again
Tempered by time itself
Not of essence lost
Pain muted
By the cry of historic winds
Love never forgotten
Or scattered to the winds

An ancient vow of love
Shines through the tarnish of time
Layered on our rings
To remind us of our truth

That our essence is destined
…to return to one another again

A love larger than life
Sweeps through our plane of life
Activating what we left inside
Waiting the grace of time
To now live this
So let it be: - Now

Trusting Love

Love opens….
Fear closes….
Trust opens….
Denial closes…
The heart knows…
The mind questions…
Love unites
Fear separates

…trust what you are brought into your life, is the learning you need in that moment. Open your heart to the healing lesson contained within. Open your soul to transformation. Open your mind to renewal of ideas.

Invocation

I AM opening, opening to your love
I AM opening, opening to your touch
I AM opening, opening to our truth
Our loving connection made manifest

As God brought you to me,
I rest my heart on the altar of our love
Unconditionally, I open to our love

Beloved one, I ask,
Rest your heart on the altar of our love
Unconditionally allow the opening of our love
When this entire world falls away
I know you will be there, and I for you
Eternally my twin essence, merged again

Healing the Twin split

At the time of the original split, the masculine energy became more of this aspect, and the same for the feminine. After thousands of years of disconnection we are now faced with the gap that needs to be bridged in order to heal the split and reunite once again.

As the masculine and feminine attempt to merge once again as one, there is a remembrance of the original split and the blame. The blame actually repels the reunification, so a space of unconditional love, allowance, and a remembrance of the innocence of the original love is needed in order to overcome this block. That energy block can be dissolved over time, but to consciously work on it is a gift from the divine temples of love: - one we wish to share with you.

At essence, you're Twin Essence and you are one. An additional complication to heal is trying to maintain one's sense of self, as to dissolve in the other is natural. As the split occurred at the beginning of time, there is also a temptation to want to keep and not share your journey and all the gifts it has given you.

If you hold this space whereby the polarities of the sexes merge in the space between you. Then allow that merger to come closer and closer to your aura, eventually you may allow this within and encompass a complete merger between you and your twin. It is a case of building the trust once again. Knowing that you are one, and not being afraid of the magnificence of intensity that connection creates.

Once you get closer to the physical body space, the heart and soul will ignite with pure joy that you have found one another. It is easy to lose this space and return to fear. Hold the space and ground it within the solar plexus. Forget focus on your individual self and anchor it for your twinship. If you are having trust issues, just allow your twin's energies to unite as far as you are able. Know in time you can build on this.

The Twin Essence energy is sufficient to heal the world of all fear and it is time for as many Twin Essences to find one another as possible. I feel as though I have been on a very long journey to learn enough to be able to meet and be with my own twin. All of my previous relationships have been to give me an understanding I now have to meet and greet my twin.

Filaments of the love body

At the time prior to the separation of the Twin Essences, they were connected by a love body. The love body had very fine filaments of the highest possible potential for love, and the sacred expression of love honouring of divine sharing. It contained all of the knowledge of both souls in respect to their union, their being as one.

See Original Love Glyph 11:- this will assist you to know of the truth and work on this truth to reveal the frequencies and patterns of that love. We are here to uncover and resurrect the original pattern. Without going back to retrieve the original pattern of your love Twin Essence, how can you go forward and develop greater love through the healing of the original separation?

I feel very honoured spirit have given me such a sacred blessing to unfold, and the gift to heal with my own twin essence. To receive these deep and profound insights and healing directives – melts my own heart back into the divine oneness of the sacred love liquid light manna that flows unhindered through mine own heart pathways.

Exercise:-

Feeling the Sacred Love Liquid Light Manna flow of the heart. Feeling this in relation to your essence. Anchoring that true love frequency through your being, on all levels.

For the complete and comprehensive healing of the original separation, it requires:-

Relinquishment of the ego. The ego will urge you on to protect yourself at all costs, including the cost of losing your loved one, and repeatedly doing so.

Movement into your own original innocence – so that conditioned patterning does not get in the way of the healing and growing connection.

Requirement to be your naked self in-front of your twin essence. There is no other way to heal this rift, without complete openness and honesty.

Remember – you are likely working on the exact same issues of vulnerability. Recognise the mirror. Acceptance of one another is paramount –
YOU ARE BASICALLY ONE, NOT TWO PEOPLE.

When you ascend – you will ascend with your twin. The time to close the gap of differences is now. This is very important work to accomplish. As you heal your partner, you heal yourself. As you heal yourself you heal your partner. There are many benefits of meeting and pairing with your twin, that you may consciously work more fully by having that visual mirror – not to mention also the valuable support energetically of proximity.

The chance to reach totality, whether you become life partners or not. Loving your twin is loving yourself.

Balance is needed at this time.

Twin Balance

As we know, the universe follows many rules ordered by the divine, that flow may continue – and balance be perfected. The Twin relationship is no exception. The original rules are to ensure harmony for both parties, and this is a Sacred Contract that was birthed as the twins birthed in love. Twin Essence is all – they are joined on all levels: - of ray, of flame, of soul and beyond. The full potential is not yet unlocked to what can be possible for growth, as the growth was impeded at the time of the twin split in Atlantis.

The current issue is one of responsibility for one another, and holding that in balance. The imbalance that occurred is for the female to be the holding station for the joint creation, and the male to be the projector into the world for such. The project should have been mutually founded, as we both carry masculine and feminine. When the twins work as one, who does what is not an issue, as there are no boundaries, and as the energies join as one, all happens simultaneously.

In order, however, to correct the imbalance now, recognition of where you are in regards to the balance is required. What areas have you been called upon to strengthen? What areas does your twin need to strengthen? What areas do you hold more than your share of responsibility? What areas does your twin carry your responsibility? Is this assisting your growth towards the highest potential for you as twins? What areas can you give your twin more support? What areas do you need more support from your twin? What do you, as twinship, need in order to heal and clear the original split, and move into your new cycle of expansion?

Personal questions may surface at this time. Relevant questions may be explored within a personal journal at this time.

Calling You: - Calling in your divine partner

My naked soul, I offer you
Unadorned, full of light
Light caressing my body, my being
Sacred in this moment
I invite you,
My soul love,
Love from above – I invoke to earth

First love, you are my first love
As I birthed from God
My beloved partner
In the flesh
Our love is to actualise
To be realised
In the physical realm

My heart, pulsates with a depth of love
…So profound
Will you join me at this level?
Where our hearts can meet
Our love has been protected in the void
Awaiting this moment
Of Love resurrection
Reuniting Essence

Fear not, for I am you, you are me

Boundaries only of this world
Yet I pray for the dissolving of these
That we can know truly
Our love completely
You and I as one
Commitment as above,
So below
AMEN.

SEALED IN THE DIVINE FLAME OF THE HEART LOVE TEMPLE. Fear and illusion may not touch this. Protected by the eternal love pattern.

Love's Duality Releasing

My love, is here for you unconditionally
My heart open, unadorned
I ask, for your heart to touch my heart
Separation dissolving
Soul connection recognizing
Itself in one another
Bonds beyond time and space
Ignite the flame of our souls

Forging our reunion
Let fear not enter in here
Let us be all we can be
Let us be in every moment we can
Let us love naturally
Never hold back
For the journey right now is ours
Our time, space and reality
Our love eternally
Fear not for tomorrow
Fear not of parting, we are One in Heart

For some the path onward will be to attract their twin essence into their life. For some it may be just to receive the gift of the healing, that they may become more of who they really are beyond the pain of the original separation.

The original separation affected both Twin Essences differently. The masculine with their projective energies and the feminine with the more introverted. Before the split, of course the balance was easy; energies just flowed between the Twins Essences. We are now coming full circle where we are called to balance the original split. I have been asked by spirit to create twelve images to assist healing the split.*

Now we must embody both aspects fully within ourselves, and reconnect from that vantage point of inner wholeness.

At the point of the original separation: - Vows were decided upon, to abstain from all that would threaten the reunion of the twin essence. It was known to be a risky venture, so this was the safety valve. This vow affected each of the twin essences entire being, colouring it, and of course deeply impacting any other relationships of any nature.

For many, the search for this profound connection can be all consuming. For others, they seek to heal the pain in order to continue on spiritually on their path.

There is a lot of pain stored within the emotional body regarding the split. The love is so deep and profound, even if it is denied by either party due to the fear of reoccurrence of the pain and an inability to deal with that, on the purely emotional level, the heart connection is alive and well.

If you meet your twin essence or not, know you are connected. There may be dysfunctional cordings to remove for your mutual wellbeing that will give more "room" for higher expressions of love beyond fear to become. If you would like this assistance, we can begin that now....

Clearing and Healing

If you are in a situation where you have adversely given your power away to your Twin Essence, retrieval may be the necessary and only option for both your healing.

For those in difficulty with their twin

From the shadows
The eternal rainbow highlights my mind
Rays of love envelope my soul
Singing me back home
To my soul family

Deep waves of pure spirit
Touch me with serene coolness
Calming my entire beingness
Changing my perspective
From now to tomorrow

Loving in duality
Is not loving at all
As only love of unconditionality is real
Eternal
A heart of Gold touches...

Peace now within
I take back the power I gave away

At the time of twin separation
For lifetimes had been my focus
Beyond my own evolution
Did I seek him

I tried to heal
The split that was made
That the love would not fade
I now turn
Onward swiftly
To heal my path
That individually went awry
Due to love consummation

Ego

It is purely the ego that sees itself as separate from other beings and all of creation. As we are naturally connected by heart, often in relationship problems – we see both couples connecting out of the body, as at that point they may connect without argument of the ego and individual will. It is sad to see a couple right out of their body over this, and probably miserable at not having their own spirit in their body properly, whilst the rift is being seen to by higher level beings of love and light to assist the couple.

We also think of ourselves as separate from all the corridors of time and space, yet they are all connected. With love and truth we can reach the places we need to for our soul path....

The "fight" only occurs within the solar plexus if you let the energy streams of divine masculine and divine feminine split off. If you become a divine agent for love alchemy, you will learn to keep these energies mixing as they are in the higher realms. Once we begin to need to see ourselves as separate, the barriers go up, and the duality occurs through the split of life force streams. It is actually more difficult with the Twin Essence in some respects, as you are so alike, it is human nature to pull back to inspect the differences and work out where he ends and she begins and vice versa. The answer is to keep the love flowing and the alchemical flow as one, united in love.

Remember:-

The twin connection does not need to try to love

They ARE love

Affirmation: - "We are love" –

Will assist in further and further bonding to unity.

Love Arose

There is no space between you and me
We are bound eternally
By pure light and soul
Divine marriage by God
Created – one essence
Loving is sure
Fear not the love that holds us as one
A sacred binding of the heart
By love alone
You love me, but cannot yet tell me
Hearts beating as one
To the rhythm of the universe
All hear our love
As we recognised our uniting
Inevitably true
That we came to be
One in love, eternally

Kiss of Light

Fear not, cry not
We will never part
One in union
Love is our bond

Fear not
The intensity
Of union found
A love, before we never knew

Keep glad your heart
For our meeting
Was blessed
And guided to one another

Keep your heart happy dear
In all we have had
Blessed moments of union supreme
Unconditional love
Hearts open to eternity~~~

Twin Essence Restored – Love Realised

The walls between the twin essence and the fear of experiencing the separation twice over, finally come down, through the pain of the original separation – they not only severed from each other, but in doing so, severed part of their emotional body in order to manage the split. The deep need and yearning to be together caused further soul fragmentation over time. We now see this healing. We conclude with the healing of this. Admitting and realising the love fully that they share, the soul fusion becomes possible, and emotional bodies receive healing. They recognise their long journey together, feeling at home in each others arms, they glimpse eternity within the other Twin Essence restored

~As One~

The Mirror

Once you have accepted your twin essence as a higher mirror to yourself, it is easier for deeper healing to occur within the bond (that encompasses love and the healing needed of the fear). Once you accept yourselves as mirrors of one another, the pattern that you share, that has split off to male and female polarities, then joins, and is able to clear much easier from the unity level. Just from the willingness to join on this level in all of your fears, a lot of the energy will dissipate.

The Original Flower of Love Blueprint
Meditation Infusion/Activation

Visualise:-

White Light through the back of the heart
Patterning – blueprint
White/pink coloured light, as the blueprint now spins in the heart.
View the lifetimes– without attachment during the spinning process.
Take energies up to the thymus, condensing the pattern down – and once the blueprint is within the thymus – open the blueprint back to former size.
Observe – watch the energies.

We anchor both the masculine and feminine equally within us.

To seal:-

Blow white energies into hands in prayer position.

Visualise white/pink around the hands.
Visualise blue around the body.
Anchor through time and space.
Place hands on heart or thymus (higher heart)

....and remember: - Love joins. Fear separates.

Image: - Flower of Love blueprint (see snowflake looking images)

Twin Spirit

Chapter 2

Overlit by Lady Nada and Aphrodite

"As the two become one, Life emerges from the depths of the void, creation of love to form, is birthed"

With Beloved Blessings I now bring forth:-

The Twin Spirit connection

May all beings present begin to connect with their Twin Spirit.

Let us now begin to work consciously and energetically to bring forth the manifestation of our Twin of all Twins.

May the divine love temples now embrace us in manifesting our destined love.

We now open this chapter as an extension of the Highest Love temples in the upper realms.

Introducing Aphrodite

Aphrodite will be overlighting the materials within this chapter, along with Lady Nada. Aphrodite also is featured on the Twin Spirit Cd.*see resources

The Twin Spirit is a very high level of love completion, as it has never experienced the split in a physical or semi-physical form. This love extends and flows to all.

Light of mine
Shine in my eyes
The love we share

To assist grounding your Twin Spirit onto the Earth Plane, visualise:-

Magenta pink and Cherry Red
Violet Flame and Royal Purple

When you are this close to attracting your Twin Spirit, it can sometimes be that visions/dreams/yearnings of what you are seeking – are indeed that which your Twin Spirit is already embodying, or is currently creating. As this Twin Relationship has not experienced the split, bleed through can be to the maximum, once you have successfully healed the Twin Essence split (if you have been working with the Twin Essence). When you visit places or act in your life similar to what your Twin Spirit is doing, this acts to bring you closer to the time of manifestation of your earthly reunion.

Be yourself! Will assist to attract your Twin Spirit
Clear any last karma from your other Twin Expressions
Open to love
Clear the emotional body
Clear the heart chakra – lower and higher
Act on intuitions, even if you do not yet meet, you may be passing close by

Twin Spirit Phenomena

The Twin Spirit phenomena, is also a wakeup call to unify within our own being all opposites that may push and pull us in duality.

Blueprints =

ASSIMILIATION / INTEGRATION =

TRANSFORMATION / TRANSMUTATION =

PERSONAL SHIFTS / SELF-RE-IDENTIFICATION =

LIFE SHIFT

The power is in self-unification

Assisting meeting your Twin:-

One first needs to work on oneself to attract the qualities we wish to see in another. First we must honour and love ourselves:-

Honour
Respect of Divine Feminine & Masculine
Love of Divine Masculine & Feminine
Value of Divine Masculine & Feminine
Clearance of any down –graded treatment of oneself or another
Rising above animalistic lust to true love

Balanced Creation/Manifestation through equal Love an Light

All you create must be taken through:-

Right and Left brain.
Mental and Emotional.
Masculine and Feminine.

Other Clearing:-IMPORTANT:-

Clearing love relationships from this life and past lives to make room, and a clear foundation for the new love.

Clearing all past life impediments of the joining with your beloved partner to be.

Twin Spirit Creation

The task of the twin spirit relationship is to bring the creation vision through both persons equally. It is the epitome of unity creation and also the easiest of twin relationships to bring this through in, as what you bring through immediately affects and benefits the other.

Preparation

As we prepare deeply for our reunification with our Beloved Twin Spirit, the next part of the preparation is a deeper reunification with source, and all of creation, as once we are rejoined with our Twin Spirit, a deeper connection to all of life will then occur. For this we need to be ready and clear, less any lower energy that are not of love come as an impediment. This workshop is to assist you to rejoin with your beloved, and for a hopefully, lasting union, so preparation, cleansing and purification are essential!

Facts on Cyprus

Cyprus is a country divided in ownership. Nicosia is a divided city. At Sacred Sites in Cyprus we brought together on the physical level, that which has not received joining on a manifest level yet (Twin Spirit).

Deeper Clearing

To perform deeper clearing of one's past, it involves the person that you are now, to have more light and love than in the past, for your light to be stronger than you're dark. Belief in this is important FIRST. Secondly, to then call upon divine assistance (here you may specify divine beings you feel a stronger connection to that have divine o assist with the situation). Remember, outside the earth's atmosphere, there and at this time of great change, a cleansing is happening, requiring that we t parts of ourselves, and parts we may have abandoned in the past. If during , you find it hard to hold the light, or to co-create with the divine and hold ᴜₑ ɴɢɴt together – DO shut down any multidimensional portals that were opened by this, and BREAK the energetic connection. You may do this by intent, by no longer allowing the doorway to open. We are multidimensional beings and connect to all through our extended chakra system. Our soul is naturally in unity, and will gravitate towards what it needs to clear the most. If a deep healing has come up to be addressed, know that it is needed by your soul for your life. Try to clear the ego, if you are working on the past life, of any need to be right/wrong. Also the egos need to prove to be powerful, or to be this/that, can be a magnetic pull. Feeling you must clear something or no-one else will be able – is a mistake. If you do not feel strong enough, pull out of it. Another time will do. Be gentle with yourself during any clean out/transformation stage, take the rest you need: - remember your soul chose this time to bring this up, as it felt it was safe/comfortable to do so. Make it as smooth as possible.

Twin-Spirit -- Non-dualistic Relationship

A lot of relationships are karmic, and based on a NEED to balance past life karma. They are based on who owes who what and pay back. Once this is cleared, often the relationship suddenly feels neutral, and quickly falls apart. Pay back mentality is not love. This is something to learn when wishing to attract your Twin Spirit. One needs to learn what energies will be present, as they are non-karmic. One needs to learn to appreciate living with energies that are already balanced; they just need to be grounded in this lifetime. Some do find it "boring" once karma is cleared, and feel a need to have a payback mentality. The Twin Spirit relationship is far removed from this paradigm.

Meditation

Meditate on the energetics of Twin Spirit: - Love perfection. What does this feel like and look like? What is this energy? Exploration~~~

Twin Spirit

Blame/Projection in the Garden of Eden: - Adam's projection onto Eve created the first split between man and woman. Man and woman were created as opposite yet equal partners of love, as Sun & Moon, Land & Sea – both are different, yet cannot live without one another.

Self-honouring

In order to attract our Twin Spirit we need to fully develop self-honouring. Who in your life to you answer the call to? To others demands or your God and your own divine pathway. If it is the latter, you will know that serving your own divine pathway, also serves others too, in the most incredible ways. If the former, you will most likely feel buffeted around by life, and out of control.

Ensuring maximum potential

In order to ensure maximum potential, it is important to make sure the foundation is clear.

Ask to repattern any beliefs that hold you less than your divine soul destiny for this lifetime.

Ask to nullify any agreements, vows or promises that you may have made in this lifetime or past lifetimes that are not for your highest good and part of this lifetime.

Ask for anything you have set up in this lifetime, that is out-moded re: - your soul growth, to be up-dated, and expanded upon, so that your soul growth may continue to the maximum.

Ask to have recoded any messages in your body, perhaps from past lives, that hold your body in any lesser states than your soul/spirit are vibrating at.

Ask for divine re-arrangement of any set-ups you have for this lifetime that you may have already surpassed by doing better in this life/achieving more than you set out to do or expected from yourself. Asking for this will clear away any agreements that are running on automatic pilot, re-arrange them to where your soul is at on your destined path right now. It will assist you to avoid continuing on this "just because you agreed to it", even if you have cleared the karma, and are actually finished with that lesson – then there would be no point/reason to continuing on. The other party can then continue any lessons with another if necessary, or be released also – depending upon where they are on their own divine pathway.

Finally, group agreements you may have made, and find difficult to know how to deal with, due to feeling you may be letting the whole group down, or that they might not be able to achieve the group purpose without you, etc. You may have expanded over the group purpose, or need a more evolved purpose to be given to you within the group. Just ask spirit that you are either elevated within the group if this is your highest purpose, or that you are granted permanent leave from the group if this be your highest divine pathway. In severing, it is also important to make alternative arrangements to connect to your new groups that reflect your current soul level: - I ask spirit to connect me to my new groups that are part of my new divine purpose and destiny. I explicitly ask that I not be suppressed/excluded/held by past arrangements that do not allow for the unfoldment of my new divine purpose that has been reached by new acts of light/love and/or unexpected rapid progress upon my life path. I do not allow for distraction from my past groups/agreements to interfere with my transition to what is right for me now, for my divine life path. I ask for all this to be registered with the Lords of Karma, to protect me from any potential problems regarding such. I ask for smooth graceful transitioning, and a graceful falling away of that which no longer serves me – including any links to persons/groups that are not operating at my current level of evolution. I ask this to be grounded according to divine law and devic laws.

Sometimes our bodies and soul/spirit can be completely out of synch, and cause illness from this. Perhaps your masculine/feminine balance is out of synch, which would have far reaching consequence, as both energies are needed for creation. Perhaps you are too active/seeking/projecting out into the world (masculine), or you do not act upon things enough and wait to receive/Cause energies to become stagnant by being too intuitive without the required follow-up action? (Over-usage of the feminine). If you over use the male side you may end up feeling soul-less and burnt out, and waste a lot of time going off the beaten track – and not be sure what the right track is, or how to get onto the right track. If you run a predominant energy in one area, the other may feel totally foreign to you. Ask to be recoded to your highest opposite of what you are not yet embodying. Notice how balanced you feel after this recoding. A lot of lower energy may release, so this work is good to do whilst in a relaxing salt bath, where the toxins may pour out, and then be drained away.

Last night I was shown the Twin Spirit patterning, and how their love sparks are as one, and the joining of them, to that which is ultimately ONE, not TWO souls. This is the union this paradigm to assist us to move toward and manifest. Update: - In 2008, a new energy began to flow through me, carrying a clarity and pristine quality like never before: - The Divine Twin.

As One

To time I surrender
My heart
To the ONE
I await
Time, even life,
Its meaning is different without you
For you are my key
To my own soul, and I to yours
Destined time is close
For our meeting time
For our rejoining of hearts, minds
And our ultimate soul reunion
I welcome you in
My beloved of all beloveds
No reservations stand in the way any longer
You are my truth, and I yours
We belong together, as ONE
This I request dearest God
That you now unite us in this world

As we are in all other worlds
May you join our lives together as one
In Sacred Marriage of Spirit

Some Lessons for this lifetime:-

Not to leave etheric doors open – can cause numerous problems

Lesson for this lifetime, to look at agreements, learn from the past on this, and get it right this lifetime

If there are karmic arrangements, do not allow them to be expanded upon/added to/renewed automatically. Once the karma is healed and cleared – move on, or allow the relationship to operate on a non-karmic level – that is if it is possible with the other parties.

When you are born you have a bubble to protect you etherically, but it does not teach you how to protect yourself necessarily. Ask for removal of this, and to transform and transmute any residue. Ask if you need assistance to clear anything "bad" from your past, and move on towards a brighter future.

If you are a former God/Goddess, it may be through the fall that karmically you were removed from bringing this power to the earth plane. This is often played out multiple ways – from being overpowered by others (as you cannot access your own power – but it is there), to misuse of what you do have on some level, or an apathy from being cut off from a part of your power of creation. The time is now to resolve this.

Preparation

Clearing the past pathways of the heart – so it is back to its most positive expression – ready for the twin spirit reunion.

This includes opening your heart to love and to spirit.

To clear all distortion in the energy field.

Honoring – respect in action of one's Twin. How might you show this to your Twin Spirit, of your love and adoration? What special things may you do for your Twin to physically show that respect.

Note: - It has become a distortion that to show this kind of attention to one another means that you are not showing this to God. This is a distorted belief, as God is LOVE, and to find special ways to show that love, you are feeding the LOVE ray, which is God in Action. God is also within all of us, and it is up to us, here on earth, to embody and live wondrous lives as couples and families.

cles

nd – Full – Richness

– Flow – Synthesizing

Bottom – Beginning - Empty

Soul Evolution

Seek to learn many new higher subtle soul qualities. Rosie quartz crystals will help you hold this in balance until you have embodied the qualities within yourself and stabilized this permanently.

How can you use your power? The fact that you think you are stuck is an illusion. We all have the power of I AM presence of our own higher self to move beyond. Clear any karma that need be. Be open and aware.

You will separate from that which you wish not to be part of your life, when you no longer resonate to it, or need to draw identity from it – whether positive or negative.

When you are truly fully ready for a change, it will happen. When you have established what you need from the present circumstance, it will happen, when you can truly envision separating from what you seek not to be part of any longer.

You have connected in the past, so well to the land and places. Enjoy now the processes with people.

Know that if you are ready, change can happen almost overnight.

Sometimes you may get a picture of what this would look like, but not fully trust that there is a pathway by which it will happen. Believe in miracles, and that what you need will come to you. Just be open to embrace it when it does! If you feel a lack of opportunities/contacts, this may be the hardest part. Know everything in life is a gift – a window of opportunity that shifts as the sands of time move on. Embrace fully each opportunity as it arises!

Twin Spirit – The true blessing

Twin spirit
Come to me
Envelope my soul
In your radiance

Light my heart
With the light of your soul
Embody me
As we are one

I love you
Beyond life itself
Create with me
The pathway to our Union

It is you
I have waited for
For our reunification
The time is NOW
For this to happen
No delay may come between us now
For we are to be united
In the physical
In the flesh
As before in spirit
Now in body
Physicalise our love
My dear one
That I may know
Your love expression on all planes
That are love is anchored eternally
I ask for Gods/Goddesses blessing on this
That it will transpire
Thanks be to God/Goddess.

The Greater Truth

Notice how the truth of all, of who we are is being revealed, allowing us great peace within and outside of ourselves as is reflected. As this happens we naturally draw to us, who belongs with us.

As individuals outside of our natural unified state, we are all vulnerable, and need love to once again feel the unified state. Allow yourself to be this, as a hardened exterior would just isolate oneself.

Gifts of Cyprus

The energies are working similar to an eraser, or clearing the glue that holds the problem situation together.

Regarding the recycling of energies, the process that is occurring is to complete the transformation of the old.

Black Stone of Aphrodite

We visited the Black Stone of Aphrodite in the Museum, next to the Temple of Aphrodite. We touched the stone and asked for a blessing on meeting our Twin Spirit, and proceeded with the poem in this manual. An amazing feeling alongside a true blessing of love was received upon touching the ancient stone of Aphrodite. A majestic, magnetic stone of Love.

Clearing/Healing

Begin by bringing into focus the problem you would like the clearing/healing on.
Visualise an Aqua blue ring around you, with lemon yellow ring nearest to your body.
Push problem to the outside of the ring.
Visualise silver/white snowflakes cascading inside your body, cleansing/repattering.
Now visualize a silver ring outside of the Aqua ring. Ask for Resolution/Karmic absolution if allowed. Any that are not allowed – ask for grace, ease and the swift resolution of such.
Next visualize a gold tube around the body. The tube is white inside. Then visualize any additional problems you may have, being included into the clearing. The white turns to rainbow as the karma clears.

Finishing Note:-

You CAN create anything that you believe. Your thoughts indeed DO create your reality. If you choose to live the way you have in the past, decide if you really wish to recreate that life? Or do you want, in this moment, to create a NEW LIFE? Seriously think about the thought forms that you are sending out to the universe. Seriously think about how you act out in life – is this really as you would wish to act, and to live? Are

you spending time bending to the will of others, when you have your owr
how you wish for your life to go – but you never act upon them? How .
dreams come true, if you don't act on the smaller messages of living? You need ᴜ
learn to master the smaller messages, then you will have the foundation, and control of
energy, to make BIG changes. Sometimes we are put in low key situations in order to
master the paradigm. Sometimes we are balancing karma, and are ready to move on
once we have done this. Even if the other person is not ready, you can still move on, if
you have fulfilled your key learning that is necessary for your soul evolution. Shifts
are not necessarily tied to one person, group or situation. Life is tied just to YOU. This
is why the term "mirroring" is often used. See what messages there are. It could be an
opportunity for you to stick up for something you believe in.

Ultimately we do program our own reality. If you believe everything will be late, or
happen at inconvenient times, then the likelihood, it will! Start thinking how you
would like things to happen, in your new life of LOVE and BLISS that we are
currently exploring on this level: - TWIN SPIRIT
We were truly blessed with a Joy-filled time in Cyprus!

Sites visited:-

Rock of Aphrodite – Aphrodite's birth place – Atlantean Clearing
Temple of Aphrodite – Globe meditation
Museum – housing black stone of Aphrodite – Invocation to Twin Spirit
Aphrodite's baths – Clearing and deeper connection via physical to the paradigm.

Intent

Intent Changes everything! How something looks or will turn out, dependent upon on
our type and intensity of focus will change the outcome. Even if we eat or prepare
food with intent, that will be the energy that will go into the food. Sometimes we put
too much intent/energy/focus onto what we do not like and wish to change, whereas
we need to put energy into what we wish to change. If we do not do this, we are
forgetting we are to co-create with God, as we are a spark of God, and that spark is in
the very core of our substance of being.

Due to the time of the fall, and various acts of further falling from the light that
occurred afterwards, many misused the God – Spark for power alone, power for
themselves, and did not circulate this energy back to God, but wanted to hoard the
power. Light without love, is not life at all. Light IS love, but many attempts have
been made to secure the gifts of light in an esoteric manner for self benefits, without
realising that we must grow as souls also, or the light will not be permanent and self-
sustaining. The light will go out, without soul qualities within oneself to regenerate.
Many of the fallen beings never did understand this phenomenon. Most of the time
period of Atlantis was spent experimenting with the God force energies, to become
super human, super powered. The truth is, yes you can become super human/super
powered, when you become evolved as a soul:- this then becomes natural, as God
gives you this power more and more – knowing you will use it wisely.

Infinite

The universe is an infinite flow. There is no such thing as lack, as flow is ongoing, and always follows route and replenishes, as long as you are following universal law of the gifting back to life in whatever form you are guided, you are allowing the flow in – through you – back out (in your gifting back), so it may go back into the creational void – and you may draw from life once again. Like the out breath and in breath of life/prana~

Creation

Changing the expanse of time is possible. Space and time, under experiment – contracted to make physical mass – solid form.

There are two forms of control:-

Self Control - personal

Controlling your own reality – or letting it flow.

Masculine: - tends to condense form

Feminine: - tends to open form & allow flow

The Blessing

May this blessing assist you to find and anchor on the earth plane, your true beloved Twin Spirit. Blessings flow forth from this short message. Beloved ones, I love you! ~ Lady Nada.

Present changes Future

Past	Present	Future
	Changing now will ripple out & affect the future	Metamorphosis

The energy goes out along the time lines and changes the future.

The soul is to be like the jewel.

Shift of consciousness seals healing and teaching

Invisible threads connect us to one another.

Use psychic abilities both in and out of the body, rather than just out of the body.

Many instructions were given on integration of the Twin Spirit energies: - via massage/exercise/herbal teas to cleanse/immersion and much more.

If you pull the highest pictures of reality – it pulls that reality from the astral to the higher picture for manifestation.

Karmic Fires

Visualise:-

The Black Vodial ring	}	Merging physical and divine law
Silver Vodial ring	}	
Ruby ring	-	Flesh (physical) and also wealth
Green ring	-	Gaia
Blue ring	-	Subconscious and Sea

Spin the rings in alternate directions – clockwise/anti-clockwise, and above/below around your aura/merkabah

Now State: - I break all vows/agreements/contracts to serve/be subservient/be connected to any beings holding me in karmic situations whereby I have released and cleared/fulfilled my karma. I also release any beings I hold in karmic situations whereby they have cleared their karma, but I have not.

I ask this now, and so it is.

Twin Spirit Template Initiation

The twin spirit templates are Lemon Yellow/ Orange / Magenta / Gold: - In colour Like a filigree lace or snowflake pattern – yet more complex. They are to create the new patterning anchorage for the paradigm blueprint for the new families of light to be birthed on earth. Aphrodite as an overseer of marriage, and has been very connected to the earth plane, is assisting the truth of the connection of the full spectrum of love frequencies required to embody all the aspects of true love. As a Goddess birthed from the sea, yet lived on the land, she is created carrying both conscious (land) and subconscious (sea), of Neptune (connect – sunken Atlantis - & all effects of), and Gaia (Lemuria Rising – now). She has been a Goddess to attempt to hold balance in the world via love. To take on such a task, even swayed herself, a Goddess, but this was the way to bring love back into the world, after many root races of a savage nature, sacrifice and bloodshed. Bringing back the love aspired many at that time, and many exquisite works of art of incredible beauty were created at this time. Famous artists, after this time also had inspiration from sculpture/art seen from this time in earlier history. Aphrodite as a soul has now come full circle, and she completes now, as each person now must ultimately decide to choose love. In assisting many, it created great turmoil in her own situations from the heightened energy of love being so unrecognized. This is why it is important that each individual "wake-up" in their own unique way, and choose love. You may have been seeking that love, seeing it as elusive and far. We now bring to you that love, both as a gifting, and also that you can work with embodying the templates into form and practice this in your life – how the new family of light will look. You are a way shower for the new patterning of relationships. Ground this well in your reality – Allow the wings of doves to caress you. Allow the swans of Aphrodite to turn you to grace and beauty. Allow the divine nectar of the love Goddess to fill every gland in your body – so as to be rejuvenated – and equal for the task. Now we are going to bring this through: - On the emerald ray and the silver ray, the Goddess Aphrodite comes to grace us this day: - Greetings in the life and light of all that you are, we welcome you to this ceremony on Cyprus. Many a time I have shown love and shared love, although throughout history this may be misinterpreted, in many ways – as a more sexual love. We have now reached the point in history, where it is very important for the new paradigms and templates, to come down through our body, to assist humanity in knowing what the true pattern is, for many have forgotten what is possible and there is a rift between the masculine and the feminine. We now seek to balance this imbalance now. Allow these energies to imbue into your body, into your fields throughout all levels of your being. Allow the energies to move into every cell, every blood crystal of your being.

Every part of you multidimensionally, throughout all time and space. Allow this to settle within your physical body, your chakras and your aura now, that the beauty and grace of which you are truly meant to be on earth is experienced, within your reality. You have the chance to hold this light on the physical plane if you choose this in this lifetime, now. With our assistance, we will bring this energy through to help support you in the process. Hold no boundaries to this happening. Release all blocks of this also, of embodying this in your physical fields, in your reality. Allow anything in your reality that is not part of this beauty, harmony and grace to release – and have no resistance to the releasing of such. Anything that is truly meant to recalibrate and come back into your life – will do so, with no reservation. So do not worry for that which is leaving your life, or changing in your life. Know that it is all part of the picture of what is being created. Allow the patterning to come into all areas of the glands of the body, from the brain – through the whole body. Allow the body and all levels of your being and soul, to recognise this shift that you are willing to make.

Lady Nada now enters: - and may this ceremony be completely and entirely blessed from all levels of your being – throughout all time and space, as the divine hierarchy watch upon you, the wings of the dove surround you, allow your heart to open to the wider doorway that it truly is, hold no reservation, for what is the reservation but a fear – a fear of hurt – a fear of harm. Drops of divine nectar are placed on your heart chakra, to assist this process. We have truly blessed this nectar and opened up the elements of this, that they are fully alive and awake, for transformation on all levels of your being. Now some droplets are placed on your thymus, on your higher heart, that you may learn of the higher expressions of love, beyond fear, where there is no reservation, where unity is the natural expression of life. Do you accept to take the initiation into the new templates of the family? .... (Pause for your answer. If yes – you may now move into the ceremony). A droplet of nectar is placed on your crown chakra, which you may assist to open up to hear us and to feel us. On your crown chakra you may place some drops of the oil – that it will help you to feel us and hear us, that your senses will open up to hearing spirit directly, that you may not need all of your messages from a third party. You may begin to receive your messages directly. Take a deep breath, and allow this to filter through your entire fields. I come as a merged being of Aphrodite and Lady Nada at this point. We bring the balance of heaven and earth – of love. Visualise a figure of eight, going from the left side of your heart chakra to the right side of your heart chakra. We are now blending to a more physical plane for the twin spirit manifestation into your life. Allow the new flame of love to be given into your right hand, and you will see this as a beautiful golden lemon with crimson flames around the outside. Place this flame into your heart chakra, allow it to burn there – allow it to burn off all dross, all negativity, and all your reservations of moving into the fullness of who you are. We can be the fullness of who we are in any minute – without any reservations, but many of us hold back, and never live the full expression of who we are. But the reality is that we can open up in any moment to the fullness of who we are, if we are not afraid of the consequences. But all that there is, is to open up to the fullness of who we are, and with those who are in the fullest connection also, may connect to us in fullness, that we may receive unity and feel unity pour out in our lives. Twist the flame down the body, burning the pathway to the solar plexus. As you do this, you may see a cobalt blue and violet flame. Take this all the way down into the second sacral chakra. Allow the flame to sit there, for manifestation of the twin spirit. Visualise white around your aura now, for protection, and seal in and give thanks to God for this initiation. We give thanks to God for this initiation after receiving white all around our aura for sealing. Thanks be to God. Put your hands on your thymus now. We are complete and finished and hope very much that you enjoyed the energies that we have brought forth for this whole trip, and the time of commitment to the truth. We hope you have enjoyed our company, as we have enjoyed the blessings we have bestowed upon you. Thank you and Blessings.

Let it be completed now. So be it. Sealed by all Gods/Goddess of the highest absolute supreme light of the One God.

Reality Transforming Meditation

Visualise a Globe, dripping liquid light: - Gold and Crimson Pink
Visualise your current reality inside the globe
Visualise your reality beginning to heal and change to the reality of your dreams within the centre of the globe.
Visualise contracts and agreements that are causing the current reality not to shift, now releasing out of the globe.
Ask for any other agreements that need to be cancelled at this time, also to release from the globe and dissolve the agreements.
The globe now glows pink from the healing of the paradigm you are transforming.
NOW live YOUR DREAM!!!!
Note: - Meditation was channelled at the Temple of Aphrodite, Cyprus.

May love come your way
Touches of Love's breeze move through your soul
Open your heart
So you know the way
A love so strong, by nature binding
By the sheer intensity of heart
Is soon to be explored
Cupid, open the way to the meeting of souls
Destined to be as one

The Poetry

Chapter 3

This chapter was shared at a live workshop in Maldon and in Glastonbury. The written part was the collated love poems, and the energy release from the reading of these out loud, but the workshop itself was not recorded. This level represents the first two levels: - Twin flame and Twin ray.

Twin Flame Love

A love like no other
My heart feels the call to you
The memory of separation rises, deeply carved in my heart
For I am you, and you are me
One together throughout all time
The tears of our parting touch my soul through our lifetimes
As it is upon us once more seeking the union
The angel wings wrap around me
Comforting me, reassuring me
The time for our complete union will soon be
This solace I seek
Wide eyed in innocence and total love
For you are the one
No other can take this place
My heart reaches out to you, deeply longing to heal the separation
To be in total union
Yet I know painfully so, I must await divine timing
One day our hearts will be as one, In Union, in all
All that we are will be forever more

Soul Flame

The pain of separation
Echoes out beyond my heart
The universe hearing my cry

Love realised in my life
…and taken away again
Leaving me empty, but of memories
The feeling of you near…
…in my heart and soul

Why leave so soon?
I hardly knew you this time
But my heart sings of lifetime after lifetime
Sharing love, sharing bliss
Contentment abounded

When will the separation end?
When will I meet you again?
When will I not be torn from my love?
…but grow and unite
Two flames burning in the night

My Soul mate, My Soul love

More than I can imagine
I missed you my love
My heart full in love
And in the pain of missing you

You touched the very core of me
Your gentleness touched my soul
When you reach for me
You know my soul

I felt pain like never before
On leaving you today
Feeling the depth of knowing you
I welcomed you within

You touch my heart..........
You touch my soul.........
I feel the Love.......
I feel the Pain........

Soul mates reunited in memories abounded
A myriad of feelings, the bliss and the pain
…until, my darling, I see you again

Into the flame

Into the flame, my heart is alight with loves endurance
Destiny's fight
How could I be without you?
When I am one with all.
When I am with you, I am in your soul
You are in my soul
Merging relentlessly, igniting destiny.
Loves flame burst forth
Can my heart endure it without you?
Come to me, into my life
Share in loves delight.
I am truly yours, as you are mine
As one,
Hand in hand
With the creator of all.

Distance

Distance is yet an illusion
When we are joined in heart
A part of us
Reaching beyond
Guided by destiny
Beginning to unfold
What does your heart tell you?
As lifetimes together
Are brought before your mind
The souls are illuminated
As the sparks once divided
Reach beyond the separation
To join again

True Love – Real Love

True Love
Waits behind the door to heaven
Where my angel love is
The true love of my heart

My desire burns within my soul
Yearning our union
To be as we once were
The candle lit
The flame burning

Our love unites us
In perfection of all that is
We belong in sacred union
Of our love

A teardrop falls
My eyes wide in innocent love for you
My heart waiting for our union

I hold out my hand to you
And through the mists you step
Into my life
Where you were always destined to be

Will you take me as I am?

Will you take me as I am?
…and all that I am
Deep into your heart
To shine the souls light in illumination
Of Divine Love
Will you take me as I am?
…and all that I am
To the depths of your heart
…your life, your being
…and all that you are
..And say you are mine
Will you take me as I am?
In eternal Union,
United by Light
Promises of Eternity...
..A love bound of truth and eternal love everlasting
Love that burns like no other love
For you are the one true love
My heart, my life, my love.
So strong nothing will ever overcome it.

One Heart

One heart,
Let your heart reach mine,
Through the rain
Through the storms
The entrance to my heart,
You have found

Love,
As the sun enters near, you are here,
In my life, in my heart
Reaching from afar, coming near

I Love You,
In everything I do,
You are part of me, part of it all,
As one, together in Unity.

Heartbreak from our distance,
From our parting,
Please let it mend,
Let's go on, be together,
As it was destined to be.

Merge with me,
Let our flames become as one,
Eternally, burning bright, burning love,
Throughout all time,
Break the chains of Eden, find paradise again,
In our lives, in our hearts.

I love you,
I join you as God made us joined at the start,
Let's go forward, by becoming one,
Move through the tears,
Find the paradise of love,
Open to me, for I truly want you.

A prayer to my Beloved

Blessed, Beloved,
From where you came,
To rejoin our flame,
I wonder.

Through mists of time
Galaxies away,
Spirals of universes,
You found your way!

To me, into my heart,
Like we were never apart,
Your beauty of your soul,
Cloaks my being in pure tenderness

As you move nearer,
To my life, I feel you enter within,
My space, my sacred life,
Suddenly becomes more so,
For I know I have waited for you
Since the beginning of time,
Two flames, were as one,
Now seeking reunion
In the heart of the divine,

May your love, join with my love,
May the mystical spiritual union,
Finally take its spiral,
Into becoming the Beloved of the Beloveds
Now beyond separation,
Beyond intrusion,
For those that God brings together again,
No man must separate or hold apart
And so be it.

Twin Souls

When I see you there, my heart turns to you,
Yours to mine, in bliss divine,
Together on earth, I found you again,
To search no more.

You pull at my heart, stirring my mind,
On our ancient memories of our true connection,
As love twins' soul.
Parted we were, to start our journeys
Not together that time.
To ancient love rekindled,
Let it touch your heart, your soul.

Will you let the flames unite?
Burn together once more?
Will you let your heart feel our love?
To its core?
Will you let the fire of our twinship?
Fire your soul once more?
Our hearts as one.

True Love.2.

I have waited lifetimes to return to you,
My beloved one,
To feel that familiarity, beckon me home,
To be as one with you again.

Two flames, sharing one true heart of eternal Union,
Divine Twin's, Divine Flames.

Many times, I have reached out for you,
Wondered where you were,
Wanting to hear your voice,
To remember your touch.

Our love has deepened,
As the pain of separation carved deep into my heart,
Mirrors of Union Divine,
You and I as one,
Ever glowing flame, of True Love.

On the wings of love

On the wings of Love, we glide, along the heavenly stairway,
Into the heart, Of the Rose, of Love.

Ocean deep is my love for you, clear as the sky...
..Is knowing I love you.

Purer than Diamond crystals, my heart beats,
As the deep core of the earth.

We met on Earth, Temporarily bound
By it's restrictions, but our love
Overcomes even death
Death will never part us

Returning Back Home –
My true Home

Open the doors
To the kingdom of heaven
See how my soul soars
To yonder
See how my heart sings
The chorus of angelic choirs

Peace, eternal peace with the creator
Illuminated suns, illuminated moons,
Cosmic galaxy
As I glide by
On my journey home

My beloved, by my side
My true Love
My soul partner, my twin flame,
From one flame did we begin
Destined to rejoin
Eternal divine flames of reunion

Love is ALL
Your journey taught you, on earth
To breathe love, to cry love, be love.

Love Reunited

Crystalline waves
Crash on the shore
To my heart
Our love joins us
To show us bliss of love
After many lifetimes we meet again
With joy of reunion will remain

Come into my life

How I have missed you, yet not met you,
I invite you into my life,
To share days where our love blossoms,
Of sweet surrender to our gentle love,
My heart igniting for you
My soul calling for you
Enfold me with your presence

You are the one that I await:-
Our sacred love unfurling,
Exotic memories swirling,
Of love through our soul journey,
Our hearts awaken to the truth,
That we are to be together forever more

The hollow that awaits you
Was carved when missing you
From our first separation
I await our beloved reunion.

My heart burning of the pain of missing you,
My soul yearning for our reunion,
To be as one, once again.
I know the time is now so near,
I wait so patiently for our love,
As I hope you do too.

Destiny swirling, the clock of time moves us to one another,
Jubilant emotions, soul energy rippling through us,
We are magnetised together,
All elements are now in place,
Our meeting is called, to our manifest place,
Your heart in mine, mine in yours
As it was written to be, one eternally.

My Heart

Does my heart betray me?
Or is it you I am feeling
The tears in my heart
Are calling you.....

You resonate to my soul
Boy I want you near
In my heart, in my soul

My heart beats faster
Knowing you are wanting me too
I am looking for you
I need you in my life tonight

On my breath, on my life
Oh....I need you here
With me

Babe, you are my love
My heart
And I feel you
Deep inside my soul

On my breath
Inside my soul
Joining in my life
Come into my life

Love is a mystery to be lived, not analyzed

Reaching Through

When I seek,
Within me,
The times you touch,
Through the very heart of my soul.

I reach out
Touch you almost intimately
You reach out and touch me
...but only in our dreams~
~~~~is it real.

Be....come on and be with me
Night and day~~
Don't hold back
Let your heart be with me
....through eternity~~~

When I'm cold
You reach through every part of me~~~~~
Warm my heart~~~
Melt me to the core of my soul.
Forever~~~and a day~~~~

I love you
Can't you see~~~what I wouldn't do for you?
Day and night,
Sun or rain,
..I just want to be with~~~~~
you~~~~again~~~

Finally

Finally, the heaven sent love,
God has sent me,
The jewel in my heart awakens
Painful sadness of when we were apart.
The sorrow fills my soul
As the promise of our reunion
Weaves into my heart and my dreams.

I have longed for this moment
Of our uniting once again
To feel the love of all
To feel a gift of human love
To feel love in the human form

From Troy I awoke to you
Feeling your soul
Yearning the merging
Of our hearts and our souls

My search is now over
Our total union I seek once more
As it was in our ancient life together

Let our souls become one
Let our hearts unite
Let love's flames burn high
In the middle of the night

I was born to be with you,
Will love you until the day I die.

Let our cycle complete
Understand our love, I pray, know who I am.

Let us heal our Karma,
Let us all be together this time,
Let us overcome all barriers,
Let us speak the same language.

Let our love reincarnate,
As our souls have,
As the souls of those of Troy have,

Let our purpose together this time now be revealed,
Let no boundaries come between us,
Let our unity of love
Heal a thousand races,
Healing the past we created,
Saving the love we lived and died for: - and loving once again.

My Soul

The angels by my side
Never let me fall
Embraced by their warmth
Secure by the divine

Always a chosen one
On a path that is blessed
My treasure is within my soul
My heart is in paradise

My love is God's
From God to everyone
Here to learn harmony
And balance all extremes

In my other levels
I knew loss
Heartache carved too deep
This time I must balance
And see what's here for real

My beloved and I are one
Just waiting to realize
Our love is already in balance
A merger of divine union

Our time draws near
I feel him close
Our love is special
Soon will be time to meet

I know the time is near
My faith total
…that he is the true one
For this life

Where is he?
I feel, I prepare
Knowing in divine timing
Guiding us by God
Blessing our earth union ~ endlessly

Alchemical marriage
Male & Female
Together we are one
The jigsaw finally completes
As he, the final missing piece arrives!

Finale

My heart is breaking
Waiting for you, every time
Anticipating when will you come into my life

You are my heart
The love I know
Will fill me inside
I know, when I've found you

In the distance
I caught a glimpse of you
The truth rang through my soul
A joy I've never known before

Is it really happening?
I've waited for so long
Finally you are here
Together as one

Ying and Yang blending
Merging endlessly
A love that was so awaited
A love now fulfilled
Man & Wife

Happily Ever After

Each morning I rise…seeking you…
…but you are not there
Seeking your sweetness~~your eternal loveliness~~
Aching for you and all that you are

No-one and nothing…Can seem to fill this space
That I left inside of me…For your love embrace
Longing – turning to pain
When will you return again?
Don't wait too long…

Felt like a chasm between you and me
A high rope bridge, to end the fantasy
I held out my hand, you held out yours
Hearts uniting, the blessing is yours

Wrapped around in your love
Your are finally mine
My bravery paid
Brought you to my life
"Will you marry me" (he said)
His beautiful eyes adore me
"Yes, and forever" (I reply)

~Our fairy tale concludes~~HAPPILY EVER AFTER~

I Love You (with all my heart)

With this heart
I love so true
Following you
To the eternal realms
Heaven is in our reach

Hearing the beat of my heart
As the heartbeat of the earth
With the pulse of your spirit in heaven
Cascading streams of love
From heaven to earth, earth to heaven
Our love transcends it all

Brighter than the greatest star
Our love came from afar
And is yet to reach our paradise
For you I wait
The eternal clocks of life tick on
I wait to hold your hand

In dream time I reach out
Comforted by your presence
Wanting and longing for your touch
One day soon, I know, you always tell me
This I know
But still, later seems like forever
When I need you now

Human is my frailty
This I cannot hide
My longing is human
While my spirit feels you there
You're shining light into my soul
I miss your love in human form

Forgive my weakness
I wish to transcend
But my love is so strong
I cannot contain
The pain I hide inside
Just greet me, be by my side
Until we are rejoined
Never to be parted by dimension's gate

This life...

I'm still in love with you
Didn't know this could possibly be true
After all these years
Did my heart ever leave?

Tonight my heart is alight
Allowing myself to see you there
In the inner rose of my emotions
Did you ever leave?

The flame still burning
...never went out
Illuminating Suns and Moons
Radiating in the sky above

My path since
Has been varied and wide
All lessons tried
My being expanded
Yet my love did not fade

A ring in the Turkish sea
A ring on Greek land
Did we pay our price?
Of our love
From a divide
That was past-life?

Will our hearts truly heal?
From our hope
That seemed to die
Can we move on?
From what we lost
Without false pride?

Can our hearts become available?
To the one that is true?
For now, my beloved one
I need to be with another
The one that is true for me now
For my life, this life

Key of Love

Birthed of Light
Our beloved entered this plane
Love flowing~~~
Grace imbued our plane

Breath of Life
Entered our hearts
Breath of Life
Flowed the waters of the Earth

Fear dissolving
In majesty
Of God's grace
Becoming one
Through the doorway
Of Love

Be unafraid of Love – let the light in – shine your love to the world~~~
I AM love – You ARE love – We are Love

You are I

You are me
And I you
Another expression
Yet at soul: - same

Feminine of masculine
Masculine of feminine
Just another expression
Of the same soul identity

Both dreaming, awaiting meeting
Hearts aligning, preparing reunion
My heart is awake for you
Loving you forever

Just as you are
I will take you
Into my arms
To live as one

You are who I have waited for
To merge all who we are
To join our lives as ONE
Come to me, beloved One

Many moments of sharing ahead
A blissful life of love
The rose of love
Encompassing us

Angels guide us
For our earth meeting
It is time
To join on earth, as it is in heaven

Love of my Life

Light of mine
Shine in my eyes
The love we share
Oh Love of my Life
Enter forth
To join my life

Light of my Light of Creation
Heart of my Heart
I saw you there
Waiting for me
Through the veils
To your love I succumbed
Relentlessly in divine love passion
The depth of this love
Is why I have waited
For this love cannot be surpassed
This love only you and I share
You are my treasure
That I seek
Upon the earth plane
To rest my head upon your shoulders
And my heart in your heart
My soul next to your soul
Intertwining in Yin/Yang majesty
Our love is endless
Our love is eternal

Eternal Marriage

Your breath
The same as my breath
One heart beats
Eternal marriage
Seals our love
Loving as one
You and I
One soul

The Blade and the Chalice

The cup overflows
With divine majesty
They whom rule
Grace our world once more

Heart to heart
Love reigns
Light reigns
Thy kingdom come

Drink from the Chalice
Elixirs of Eternal Life
Flow through my being
Transforming mortality into the immortal

Enter Christ and Bride of Christ
Whom welcome me home
Immortal drops of heaven
Enter into my soul

Since the beginning of time
I have waited for this moment
For their love to imbue Earth once more
My heart and soul rest at peace in Sacred Union

The bloodline finally revealed
To all who wait
With the peace of the dove Shekinah
Know true divine timing
Opening the seal of the heart
To dimensions untold

Finale Blessing

May love come your way
Touches of Love's breeze move through your soul
Open your heart
So you know the way

A love so strong, by nature binding
By the sheer intensity of heart
Is soon to be explored
Cupid, open the way
To the meeting of souls
Destined to be as one

By love you will find me
Open the doorway to your heart
For it is there you will find me
Reach out with your heart
I will be there to take your hand
Leading you back "home"

Divine Wedding – Sacred Union

Blessings bestowed upon thee
For the moment of divine sacred union is upon thee
Oh beloved souls of remembrance
Of soul embrace
Twin Flame
Birthed as One
Returned to reunite as flames
Of ecstatic union
Love sublime

How mine heart trembles
To witness this union
The tears of remembrance
Drop gently down mine own cheek
As my heart opens to thee
For the moment of your union
Embraces all unions
Your flame
Lights the flame in all Twin Flames
Sacred Union

To my love

Light of mine
Shine in my eyes
The love we share
Light of my Light of Creation
Heart of my Heart
I saw you there
Waiting for me
Through the veils
To your love I succumbed
Relentlessly in divine love passion
The depth of this love
Is why I have waited
For this love cannot be surpassed
This love only you and I share
You are my treasure
That I seek
Upon the earth plane
To rest my head upon your shoulders
And my heart in your heart
My soul next to your soul
Intertwining in Yin/Yang majesty
Our love is endless
Our love is eternal
Your breath
The same as my breath
One heart beats
Eternal marriage
Seals our love
Loving as one
You and I
One soul

Love is

Love is, unique, mystifying,
Warm in its union
A joy, a celebration
A heart link throughout all time

Love never disappears
As love is eternal
Love embraces
Love caresses

Love bridges
For love is the bridge
Love knows
…and is ever present

Love is the mystifying force of life
That knows no death
For the light of the angels caress
Moves one form to another

…know you were loved
With a gentle love
You're being brought a heart awakening
Opening to love unending

Each form one embodies
One learns anew
One breathes anew
Life after life…

….Do we become, and ever in the process of becoming….

You are but in another dimension
…through the door you stepped…
Radiant in your soul form
…let slip the silky body of physicality
…ready to begin, anew….

You

The balmy sweet summer breeze
Of a late August night
Weaves whisps of caressing kisses
From the ethers
To my soul

Your soul and mine
Together
..Alone
At last
Is more than I could wish for
Everything I wait in hope for

The immense wanting of you
…breaks open
The secret most inner doorways
..To my heart
..That was locked
…by another

I can do no more
Except love you
Unconditionally
Waiting the return
…of my love of all loves
Under bridal wings
And sacred bonds
Two birds of paradise
Join us above, as one
Married on high:-
And as it is above, thus must BE below

The Songs of Sacred Union

Chapter 4

Pure love: - Part One

Pure love lives in the moment
Pure love does not know time; it reaches out for love uniting
Pure love does not hesitate, or think ahead - for to be pure love, you must love with all that you are in that moment.
Hesitating love is a past paradigm that no longer lives in my reality.
I now love in a new way, ever radiating, never holding on: - for a tomorrow that may or may not come.
Join me now - if you can light your heart to the same space as mine.
Tomorrows promises are like raindrops in the ocean that could be lost - or change form.

Nerida - Soul Unity

Every time within my heart
I was seeking you
Now I know what feeling complete is
..Joining eternally
My heart has ignited
The memory of our love
Burning deep in my heart
I yearn to be near you.
Unifying~~~
You are mesmerizing~~
My being.
Beloved, I want you endlessly
Eternally.
Destiny's arms
Cradle us together
Reuniting our souls
Forever~~
More~~~

The heart doorway opens

Is this really happening?
That you must go?
Lifetimes of waiting
…and no goodbye possible?

Thank you, for opening the doorway
To my heart
Without you, I cannot do what I could before
Divine balance has shifted

Must I really say goodbye?
Or will swift relief follow
My prayers to you
From up on high, follow you

Your deep soul gifts not fully discovered
Your love, your purity
Held high
Divine plan supreme

Could this really be taken?
Trying to recover
For days
All we had

Where are you?
Archangelic protection I seek
For your soul, for your body
May your divine plan realise

Frozen tears in disbelief
Now flow freely
From my heart, from my soul
To God: - your safety I petition
Forever your soul wrapped in Golden light supreme

Soul Radiance

Stars in paradise of destiny guide my return to our love
Swiftly my heart awakens -acutely aware - you are the one
I waited so long for
Passionate love ignites the flames within my heart
Old whispers of yearning reunite us, by your word
Radiating love, burning in my heart
You found me, you knew it was me
Instantly you were seeking to rejoin our love
I lingered hesitantly, from waiting so long.....
Words of recognition on my letter to you...
..Seeking your forgiveness for hesitating with you.
Many came.....~~~Many went...~~~
How was I to know?
When I did....I couldn't find you.
Find me again....swiftly....I'm counting on you.
Trust me, my darling, for our love is true.
For: - I love you beyond time and space

Soul Blessings

I've awakened to our memory
A love so fond...
Of cherished memories
Of sweet blossoming love.
Will my love take me to you?
I sit alone, wondering...
Will we complete?
The joy and the pain:-
Will I see you again? If only I knew.
I'm ready for you.
I close my eyes and feel you within
When can I open my eyes and see you there?
Within or without
Our love's a blessing
I wait for you, my honey
For a marriage made in heaven.

Will destiny guide you back to me?
Will your heart call me back to you?
Will, in time, our love be realised?
Can I come to care for you?

Soul Merge

The breath of my heart
Escapes out to reality
Uncertain
Innocent
Eyes mirroring the pool of destiny

Fire breaks through the heart
Emerging destiny
Hearts love let lose
Finding you
Merging –AMESHOI

LEAISHA, MEINAININ, QUETENITAN
MIANANIN. LEITUN.QUESHENAIA
MAIAITENIEA.

I love you beyond paradise
Rising higher
Flames burst to soul merge
Merging in paradise
Fires rising higher
Soaring in love's flame

Soul Love

Loving you
Is the sweetest part
Of living this life

Loving you
For you are
Another part of who I am

Loving you
Extends my realities
You bridge my horizons to infinity

Loving you
You are in my breath
You coarse through my living reality

You enter in
In, my heart and my mind
Through the doorway to my soul

You open my heart
You open my soul
Chains of limitation are breaking

In our eyes
We are one
Returning to where we belong
~ ♥ ~

Soul Fusion

Softly
I come to you
Reach my hand
Open my heart

Gently you take me
Embrace me
Merging deeper
Souls fusing

Unfolding
In your arms
Flowing
My heart, like a river

Whispering
Words of love
Ecstasy
Blending our souls
As One

In your eyes
Shines the message of love
Become mine
Tonight, forever,
Eternal

Soul Flow

Breathe of life
Breathe one love

As the breathe comes through
The heart of the loved one
Opens divine springs
Of soul source within

The door opens within
To the sacred place within
The heart tenderly recognising
Union of love
Merging to unity

I have loved you since the beginning
Before our souls became form

Heart to Heart
I loved you through Galaxies, time stairways

I loved you from the void
I loved you in the light
And my love shone through the dark

I have loved you from my mind
From my soul
From my heart
From my spirit

Souls as One
Belonging....
Engaging, Igniting, Merging...
Reunited in Bliss

Returning

Find your way home to me
In my arms you will find your home
~~beloved
You and I are one.

You~~~ are my piece of heaven
You are the missing piece to my heart

I hear your voice on the wind
Caressing me, calling me home
The language of the heart
Calls me closer to you
And all that is true

You and I -
One life
One heart
ONE~~~~~~~~~

True Love – Part Two

True love feels the heart beat of life, in the ocean of love,
True love allows the flow to choose where it goes
True love knows no fear, because in love there is no fear
True love encompasses all, knowing we are all one and separation is just an illusion
True loves lives from the heart, knowing the heart of our bodies is the mind of God,
True love reaches out, radiating love wherever it goes, knowing that it reaches much
further than your sight believe,

The love you just sent out, reached someone's heart, through their heart, it went to the
stars, the stars let it flow through to all galaxies, universes, and from there it went to
the central source of creation, and into the HEART OF GOD, Who is Love.
We are Love, we only need to be who we are, and we will be that which we search
for.
Let us each be love, and unify in our hearts, and let the love of all creation flow from
all to THE ALL THAT IS.
I AM THAT I AM.

Love

As love finds me,
My heart melts to bliss
You~~~and I~~~are One.
Where-ever I am, you are too,
For you and I…
Are One…

Never thought heaven was so easy to reach
You found me
Now, I can be
Truly here

Love flowing, overflowing
Love going to you
My beloved
My true one
I love you.

My waiting is over
You are with me
My beloved one
My star of paradise

Heaven in my soul
My soul flowing to God
Flowing to you
My essence, my heart, my beloved
My Love.

Your sweetness
Opens my doors
Now: - no doors, no walls
Love supreme,
Light supreme

My love song to you.

Divine Devotion

Divine Fire ignites
Memories returned
I recognized you
Heart to Heart
Soul to Soul

My love, precious one.
Love soaring
Heart flowing
Joined in Bliss
Reunited across time
Past lives swirling before us

Sacred flowers adorn us
Sweet love imbues us
Joining,
Loving,
Sacred Uniting
Moments of Love
Forever written in the stars

Twin flames joined in body
As in spirit
Destiny fulfilled
Christ and Mary returned
Love recognized, never to be denied again
7 flames of Heaven
Join the 7 flames of earth
Love ruling, love supreme

Deeply Connected (To You)

The pain in my heart
Breaks my soul
Why my love
Did you go?
…and not let me know
…your reason to leave?

Once cherished memories
Now ingrained in pain
Once a love that blossomed
Wilted in pain
Of my tears

The beauty of our union
Lit my life anew

The love for you
I still hold
The flame within
My bleeding heart

Why separation again?
When will I feel you again?
Sadness imbues
Where love used to rule
Tears now reside
As my heart cannot hide

A deep love I still feel for you
Awaiting you to renew
Is it not the time or place?
Why won't you give it space?
Darling please join in spirit,
…heart, mind and soul.

Awakening

A thousand years sleeping
Awaiting you
Living in a dream
My heart asleep

You return
Your heart open
Flowing
Awakening my soul

Remembering....love
Transformed in a moment
Your touch
Melting my defences

Feeling alive again
Unafraid of love any longer
Love blessing my life
Your love awakened me

Chapter 5

Divine Twin

Heralding a New Twin Love Paradigm

Divine Twin

At this time of great, great change, a beautiful new opportunity is arising. The highest love expressions of beloveds have been unable to birth onto the planet, due to the energy of duality – which has made it difficult to conceive the highest love from the radiant realms. It is this love that has not been conceived before, that we will usher through on this beautiful radiant day of 17th March 2008.

Throughout this day, a blessing of light and love frequencies never before birthed onto our planet, overlit the workshop. We anchored the new paradigm for the light of life – the love in action, the love in embodiment, as only known before in the higher realms. BY this ignition of light/love infusion, so you shall attract the beloved who is a match for this frequency, and who indeed is one you know so well from the unified universes.

It is with great love that spirit introduce this to us, and know that you are ready, if you resonate to these words, and that likely you have been preparing for this moment of anchorage of the perfected love expression of all that is.

This love is what some may call TRUE LOVE, yet not many know of what this truly encompasses. True love, is real love, and this love can never fade, or become disenchanted. It can only grow, evolve, and has great purpose.

This Chapter includes: - The Sea of Love Codings and Pure Unity Codings

The energies of Divine Twin

Impeccability in form. Impeccable thought, focus, feelings ~

This is the healing ray that requires total surrender to all that is old in your life, and no longer who you really are, and holding you back. Open up to your magnificence.

Ecstatic heart opening

The veil that shrouded the Divine Twin, through this paradigm – is finally lifting, to allow for an ecstatic heart opening that was unknown to humankind before. The timing is perfect dear one, in every way, and not a second before were you or humanity read to embrace this ecstatic loving of both yourself and your mirror – your own dear Divine Twin.

How many times do we choose a contrast, "just for a change"? Instead of embracing our true match? How many times do we believe that this strengthens us? Is this not what the "medical world" believes to be true with vaccinations? But why educate the body to fight? When the body really just wants love, peace and light? Humanity has so much to learn about embracing love, but finally we are here, and we are imparting to you the opening. Dear reader(s), you are the vehicle for the grounding of the rays of true love unto the earth plane.

When you say, you do not know, sometimes it may be a lack of confidence to manifest it, and it will just spin back out and up to spirit, until you are ready to manifest it.

Awakening and enlightenment is the realisation of your full potential, the opening to all possibilities of who you are. Sometimes we delay and put on hold part of our being that dearly wants to express and live itself out in this dimensional reality. We do this for one reason or another. It limits us, and stunts our potential growth. Unless we live it – we cannot realise and therefore see it, become it, on this dimensional level. It will then remain a possibility and pure potential, until such time as we decide to give it the time, space, energy and attention that it needs in order to birth and unfold in our physical life. Spirit IS pure potentiality. On other dimensional levels we create very differently.

Unless we give time and attention to our higher self, we cannot fully truly know of our soul divine blueprint, which is our map for navigating this lifetime. We no longer have an eagle's eye overview of life that assists us to steer our path smoothly, if we do not listen to this part of our being, and regularly tune in.

We can steer our lives, or we can accept the life view of another, and another, but either way, we are still choosing. Even in apparent neutrality, we have still chosen that state. We can never NOT make a choice, for even this – is in fact – a choice in itself. The decision to not choose.

What guidelines do you want for your life?? Do you want your higher self and guides to set these, or do you want to think you have no control over your own life, and life is randomly summoning up all kinds of events and situations over which you have no control?

For clearing and healing: - the difficulty with clearing and healing is the density of the physical realm. This causes a time lapse, unless ones energy can be speeded up, along with the consciousness, the mind and the emotions, to break through the gravity of duality, to zero point, where what does not belong will automatically drop away. Part of this is the manifestation of freewill, where we were given the choice to manifest that which is other than our highest path. Often, no matter how much we think it will make us happy – it may not lead to the kind of soul growth and expansion we truly desire and energy moving in beautiful swift flow of life – feels great, whereas stagnating energy does not. To achieve this flow, we need to make decisions from our soul and spirit and allow this to manifest, no matter what.

Learn to tune in and out of what you want to create, and out of that which is leaving your life. This speeds up the process!

Notes

Anchoring our spiritual into the physical IS important, never disregard this or disbelieve the importance of this.

Equally ground physical spatial perceptions with multidimensional perceptions to assist the grounding of the spiritual. Some people become vague if they become too ungrounded, and the details of life become hazy. There is a balance here that is to be achieved!

Money or material items are not "unspiritual", and in this life – we do not have to suffer, but we are meant to be comfortable – not struggling.

Having the divine love through your twin, you can face any challenge, including things "going wrong".

Come into clarity – make a real decision to be really living and working out what that means. Anything that is old and falling away – look at it and see it for what it really is. Life is a flow and about your ability to integrate experiences as you move along this river of life, without having to "pull back" and reflect overly.

The core of who you are must be founded on your spiritual essence. If it is founded on anything else – it will affect your decisions. Do not let the man-made world have dominion over you. There is much for you to do (as yet) in the creation of the unfolding of the new world. You are a key player – that seems easily distracted at times – by the ways of the world. E.g. how does a queen exceed God?

Peace is not founded on money – but on your heart. The body is ill at ease – from past reactions to perceived persecution. This is occurring though a desire for power (at the past time), but it is more integrated now.

Past life example from workshop participant: - ((There is some karma that you have drastically been trying to resolve since the knights templar days. When you were a treasurer. The money not only went on affording the mission, but on one's own goods

– as well – to a level – over and above what was necessary. Handling money from others – designated for a purpose. For this life time it is to share, and to release the grip and allow the flow. Dear One, get the show on the road regarding your soul plans for this year and your future. Being focused on money is not what it is all about)).

When the doorway finally does open (to your new life), you will be amazed and ecstatic.

State what you want, and even if you feel like you have been waiting for a long time already – if you were to really consider – were you really ready to embrace this yet? In all its purity – without seeking old ways?

Release hesitancy about conducting your own life. Do not look to the past and second guess what you have already lived and completed. It will all fall into place – there is a bigger picture.

The universe will offer signs – if you ask. Ask that change happen with grace and ease. The transformation begins! (Through the inward process).

Divine Twin

With Love....
...the vastness of life opens
...revealing the flow
Of the universe.

With Love...
...all doors open
To your hearts dreaming

With Love...
...the fire of the soul
...is soothed...
Like a sweet summer breeze
Cradles your soul
Leads you to journeys unknown

Love is the map
To unchartered territory
...to bring to life
The hearts secret yearning
As this thirst is quenched
The soul is sublime
With the peace of spirit
As the glory becomes known

Exploration: - Belonging

The Divine Twin is to whom you belong for a partner. This belong extends to their family and friends also. Explore where you may live or relocate together to. What will be your vocation – your true work? What will your life together look like? What will your home – to anchor the love, look like? E.g. near water…etc.etc…How might you change and grow as a result of the union?

The envisioning process assists the manifestation of this higher love.

Ask assistance from your ancestors: - through the doorway of your ancestors, ground all of this in, to your life.

Things to work upon: - renewing your sense of wholeness. Renew your sense of well being.

On abundance: - when you think "shrewdly" the aura clams up. There is no need – God knows what you need and it will all be provided. Life is designed to flow.

Everything must flow forth from you – so you must become it first.

On love: - It only has to be the true love. It doesn't't have to be exotic, or passionate, although if that is its truth, it may indeed be.

Open up your feelings. Do not consider that where you are currently at is not part of love – for it all is.

Follow divine instruction for heaven on earth.

If spirit give you gifts (these can be items you are guided to buy by spirit), do keep them to protect you during times of adversity.

Know that your frequencies must stay in synchronisation.

Sometimes we work to hold such an overview of life, it can seem too abstract to suddenly begin to study one aspect, or what actually feels like one aspect, but this is, in fact – very healing to do for ones soul growth.

On partners: - For someone that truly loves you will respond always with love, and not anger, no matter how you affect them or what happens between them.

Self: - on being self-assured – allows self-integration – when you jokingly state "I don't believe it" – you reject energies that were meant to integrate and become part of you. Rejecting the gift of energies you needed to complete the transformation. Also seeing the offerings given to you – by life – as a gift from the universe – opens the heart with gratitude.

Life: - delays in life occur in response to your intent – which adjusts all of your life.

Mass society: - are too object orientated and spend time trying to gain from items, but what really nourishes us is unification in love – in our soul families and our Divine Twin – this love is what people are really looking for in the objects (but can never find there).

Allow the innocence of love to touch you and open your own innocence of spirit.

Unity

You have to complete your learning on an individual basis level before you can rejoin, and take your individual development in to its fullest state.

Begin to conceive the life you dream of…

Life as it is now, was, at one time – someone's' dream and focus, and can therefore be changed accordingly. You are free and no-one has any control over you.

Be full and overflowing with life…

Allow your life to be beautiful and meaningful and not about survival only. It is all about trust.

Recommendations:-

Red Tea (Roobois)

Past lives and Karma

Sometimes we come in to this lifetime with past life injuries to heal. A lot of earth energy and spiritual energy is required to heal the injury. Why do we wait to heal this injury the physical? If the injury occurred on the physical plane – it is sometimes better that it is also healed here, and the healing ripples through all the other levels also. Often our soul will choose to resolve and make peace on a physical level, and they wish for it to be physical – that the resolution becomes manifest. It is not essential or necessary – just desirable.

Sometimes people respond unconsciously to us from a past life, where in this life, it may have no apparent link – however, energetically it IS linked. The clearing may play out in a manner that seems disconnected and disassociated. However, from a spiritual level – it may have been balanced in the spiritual realms, so when it re-manifests as you reincarnate – the clearing necessary may be a considerably less harsh.

Sometimes it is also about building good karma, not only clearing bad karma. This is certainly the next step, once we have the space and clarity – following the clearing of negative karma.

Comfort Zone

Experiences that we continue to create are often re-created in an attempt to reproduce the same emotions that we originally experienced on the first occasion. Sometimes we will try to tap in to what we first felt, also.

Of course the ideal is to be free of the past – living in the moment, and to be happy to experience many more experiences for the first time, rather than living on repeat mode. That way, we are more authentic; we live more fully, experience many more situations, and expand/grow considerably.

Note: - You may wonder the connection of this – to the twin material. Unless we fully 100% connect to ourselves, this connection to our Divine Twin cannot come to be (not on the physical plane of joining)...

Divine Twin Workshop meditations transcript

If you would like to take a deep breath, and centre within your spiritual core, in the centre of your being. We are now going to go on a meditational journey, to the higher temple of the divine twin. This temple is in the unified universes, a place that knows no duality. The angels of this temple now come down to greet you. You will see a staircase: - they are now descending the staircase to greet you, to assist you in stepping up their frequencies of divine light. They will take your hand, and as they take your hand, your frequencies go up to a higher level. Fears and doubt begin to disappear and fade away, as you feel wrapped in their love and light and excited about the journey you are about to undertake. There is a crystal staircase right in front of you, and a light being in front of you. You begin to step up the staircase, and as you do so, all your human doubts seem to disappear, and seem to be instantly removed from the body. As you are transcending the staircase, different levels of fear and doubt begin to be released from your physical fields. You begin to hear the sounds of angels as you are going higher up these stairs, and a deep spiritual energy imbues your being. You see a soft orange glow and magenta glow coming from the top of the staircase. You are nearly at the top. You begin to remember your own angelic presence as you are at the top of the stairs. All your spiritual remembrances seem to come back to you. You are guided to a temple, and within this temple there appears to be what is like a waiting room, and you sit in this waiting room and you are asked to contemplate your thoughts for your divine marriage to your divine twin. You begin to contemplate on what this means to you from a soul level, not just a physical level, but the soul and spiritual level. Please take a moment to collect your thoughts and centre them on this.

Jesus now comes to you to call you in to this room. On his table he has his book that he opens the book of life and he turns round and shows this to you. This information is describing your journey with your twin, on these pages. Begin to take and a look and read and see if you can interpret the message. Listen to see what you hear. This is a soul message of your body and twin and the reunion of your twin ... occurring at soul level with all of this. The room is beginning to be surrounded by a turquoise glow representing your twin's energy. You Begin to feel a sense of peace, knowing and connecting on this level with you. Now the journey after reading of this from the book of life and it gives you the confidence that you know that this is meant to be. We are now taken into a room that is full of beautiful jeweled robes, and you are to collect the robe that you resonate with strongly from your spiritual call. Please take notice of colour of the robe, and how it feels when you put the robe on, how the strengths warms you. Jesus gives you a ring that you are to give to your divine twin in this temple. That which comes together in this temple can never be parted again. So this is only for those truly wishing for the permanent reunion of their divine twin. This joining is the joining of trust and absolute flow of the most perfect love in its highest expression highest form to be now made into its highest manifestation on the physical plane. We are now taken into an area of the main temple, it is absolutely beautiful, with pillars made out of rose quartz and an altar of amethyst with pearls on this altar. The most glorious jewels shine all around this temple, further elevating your energies to a higher sublime frequency. You begin to feel the journey that you've made back towards your twin; any hardships encountered begin to leave your fields at this time. So you can truly come into the centre of your being. And you see many other couples in robes that are also to be wed in this ceremony.

You see your Divine Twin on the opposite side of this temple. You see beautiful lavender lights begin to spiral between you. You feel this love and you know this joining is to be soon and to be manifest.

Under the divine over lighting influence of spirit. You see your twin who is also holding a ring that he knows is to be for you, soon to be given to you in this sacred ceremony. The sounds of heaven are a beautiful sound that is unlike any you have heard in your life begins to flow around in this temple. It is difficult to tell where this is coming from, it is surrounding the temple. Breathe out all old energy at this point in time, and take a deep breath as you prepare yourself, as your names are called to come up the divine altar of love. You are aware of how your robe feels on your body, if it's a silky texture; you feel this on your skin. You prepare yourself that you, you finally, finally joining after all this time, since our history, back where you belong with him. Or should we say forward... where you belong, where your future is together.

You kneel on this altar and the excitement is hard to contain, and high as heightened frequencies, if you are joining together. A magenta spiral comes within, through and around your hands, beginning the joining ceremony and wraps around a couple of times. The words of God flow forth from the other side of the altar, you see gold coded letters coming from the mouth of God, begins to spiral within, through and around you. You lose sense of time and space. As you forget there ever was a separation, this is no longer important to contemplate or focus this. The divine jewels within your higher hearts, a magenta colour lights up, as the ceremony is underway now.

You are just asked one more time if you absolutely desire and ready for this. For this affirmation is needed for that what you choose to originally separate, you must also decide (to) consciously to rejoin.

A beautiful angelic spiral of pearlescent white light forms a figure of eight around you. Flecks of pastel colours come through this figure of eight also. The energy heightens as the initiation comes through. Allow this to come through your body now. Absorb this frequency into your body. For it is the energy of absolute unity, that which knows no separation. That which is of total joy, total happiness, total harmony, total love, total light.

You just need to say that you are ready now.
And join your (with partner) hands together. If you are ready to say: I AM READY NOW.

Allow this energy connection to come back forth to you and join until it is flowi
a figure of eight a figure of infinity. Allow your body to be transformed by this
initiation.
.....pause....
You see a spiral staircase to your right hand side, and you begin to take this spiral
staircase together representing the beginnings of grounding of these energies. You
very slowly take each step, and as you do the step glows in violet and in cobalt blue.
More energies and frequencies transform from physical level, which you don't know
can acquire. As you descend on the staircase. And the energies in your heart, in your
high heart heighten. When you reach the bottom of the staircase, you once again place
your palms together facing each other. And you embrace doing this on the physical
level.

Lemon colour and pastel light begin to form a protective bubble around you. You see
these colours expand out in the Aura clearing all old energetic debris away of the
journey of separation. Clearing this all out from the chakras, minor and major in the
body and out of the body chakras. And from the earth plane you see the colour
platinum come up through your feet chakras, and begin to cleanse away the frequency
of doubt that is in your nervous system and now is strengthening it. White light comes
down from spirit now into your thymus chakra, filling frequency of initiation into the
chakra. All the old thought forms of separation begin to be cleared from your mind
and your emotions. Magenta light begins to surround your body, supporting and
heightening this level of love. You see a certificate before you, representing the
physical marriage should you wish to take this step.

Now close this meditation, if you put your hands in prayer position over the thymus
chakra, seal the energies in and take a deep breath. When you put your hands together
in prayer position you can see turquoise and pastel light begin to fill the entire energy
fields.

Namaste

Slowly come back into the room.

Divine Twin Workshop meditations transcript-2

Greetings this day. , we welcome you into the flow of love that we call the divine
twin. Many are celebrating this day through your earth plane, as you anchor more of
this through preparing you for this joyful re-union. Know that we are celebrating in
heavens, and preparing greater and even more even vaster spaces for you to anchor on
the physical plane. Take a deep breath now. As we tell you, this is also about you
coming into the fullness of yourself, so that you can both bring this to each other. For
how can two beings, that are both lacking bring an energy of expansion, it would be
more of the case of you bringing each other's energy out so to speak. Do you see the
reason and the point of all this preparation? Do you see why it takes this time? Do you
see the learning that you needed on the way? For once you have decided to separate
even though in this instance it's only from the physical plane level. Once you have
made that decision it joins again in different way, but its timing has become to be,
now.

The divine twin energies are ready to embody through your being in a fuller state at this time. A pathway of turquoise, pale turquoise pastel light is opening up on the earth plane this time. You walk along this path and we feel that physical substance of the ground under your feet as you walk along this turquoise path. You see some trees ahead of you to the left of you, and to your right, but the way ahead is clear. You now see the essence of the divine feminine and sleeping grace coming down from spirit, to come and anchor through your being. Through these trees you see your divine twin, waiting for you on the physical level. You look at your hand and you notice the ring on the finger from a previous meditation on the finger etherically. You contemplate the physical marriage as you ground this energy and it's paradigm into your life physically. And there are crystal blockages to be removed on this physical plane, so that those energies may come through to the physical one hundred percent and anchor. You request that these energies are being released through all times and space or levels of your being, multidimensionally, through alternative realities, alternative universes, parallel realities, parallel universes all planetary systems, all source systems, all dimensions and the void. I ask this now, and so it is. I Call in Archangel Michael to clear away all cords that are no longer of the highest good or part of the Divine Twin paradigm. Any past life contracts that you still have, or even in this life also, or future lives, that would prevent the coming together of you with your divine twin, are now placed in a pile in front of you, and you cancel all of these contracts. And slowly, slowly begin to come back into your body.

Divine Love Realised

Chapter 6

Divine Love

A SACRED LOVE OPENING - A MOMENT IN DESTINY

...As we reignite the love temple upon earth

Love realised~ Grounding divine love unto physical body

During this auspicious time, connecting remotely to where the etheric temple of love of the earth resides, it is time, dear ones, to utter the words of pure love ~ and for that resonance to heal all wounds of separation for a total healing of the emotional body to embrace your being for the frequency of the high love that is present in other realms, to now birth forth. How long, dear ones, we have waited to embrace the frequency of a love so pure~ so radiant, as the love of Christos was and is and ever will be so we offer you this opportunity to know of this, to feel this, and to embody this frequency of pure love. Like water in a desert, this river of love will quench the thirst, and feed the soul. Power, dear ones, can go two ways: - we can be the power of love, or we can love power – but only the former – unlocks the keys to divine realms of the glory of spirit. On a local, global and multiuniversal level, we invite you to take this step, as a master of light – to redress this imbalance that you may see to be evident at this site. We will anchor through the power of love, the rays of divine love – each unique in frequency and in healing magnitude, we are to be given a sacred gift of love, which opens the keys to TRUE manifestation of divinity. For those courageous souls who resonate to embodying pure love of divine, and become THE LOVE OF ALL THAT IS, I welcome you, embrace you dear ones, with white and pale silver wings – that you feel the divine resonance of a love so divine Step forth now, and allow the chains of bondage of love of power to disintegrate, and take up the divine mantle of TRUE LOVE ~ the key to open the divine doorways ONLY opens with this key We enter forth now~ to worlds so far unseen, yet to be made visible at this auspicious time,
In the radiant rays of the master Jesus,
Lord of ALL THAT IS
Namaste

We connect to the divine worlds and a special healing with the new love rays and anchoring the love temple. The power of love first birthed forth from the source of love of all that is. This love from the God and Goddess of ALL THAT IS, birthed forth sparks of LOVE of all that is. This love was powerful and emitted a light of ALL THAT IS. This light created Life of ALL THAT IS. This creation was beautiful, it was a flow, it was a dance of the universe, and the angels sang of love, and of light. All that was known was unity, and this is what love is. It is the power of this love that we will awaken within our heart chakra and our higher heart chakra on. This is the time of a great opening from the heavens of the temple of love in the higher realms~ the timing was long ago promised of this event, and this promise is honoured by the angelics. This is the time to awaken from the great sleep of the fall into duality, and to embrace ALL of the missing frequencies of creation that keep us in the illusion that we are separate from creation and the LOVE of all that is (God/Goddess). Love is an orchestra of many sounds, many frequencies~ those frequencies are the flow of life, they are what makes us happy, they are what allows us to expand, they are what heals us, what nurtures us, what makes us whole. In Lemuria, an ancient land at the beginning of time, we knew of this flow of love, we felt the power of love, we knew all of the frequencies of creation, and this powered the light to flow and to continue. Death did not exist, as the eternal frequency was intact. The missing love frequencies will be reconnected, on land that knew of the last time of when this was fully intact. Out of all places on the earth, this was the last piece of land for the light of love to go out – at the time of the fall. Therefore it must be the first place for the light to be re-lit. Without the full frequency flow of life, we do only know of a half-life. We only know of half of the reality we COULD be living. I now invite you angels in the flesh to journey with me, and to REMEMBER who you are ~ as I guide you to this sacred site, where we will relight the flame of love, in the etheric temple.

The strength of life, which was to be the power of love, but during the fall, turned into the love of power. The timing is crucial to the lead up to the ascension wave that must be birthed at this time, as mother Gaia is rebirthing. It is the time that the councils of love have chosen, as waiting for the love current to fully rebirth on this planet has been long, and waiting is no longer advisable, as beloved mother Gaia, has assisted to compensate us for the lack of love, and missing love frequencies, but mother Gaia now needs to shift in order to align with the rest of the universe, so that the earth frequencies raise. It is a time of choosing, yes, and this channeling will assist the missing love frequencies to be available, and create the much needed RETURN TO LOVE.

Anchoring the powerfully sublime energy of divine love in order to manifest this in your physical life. Clearing all blocks to becoming a being of divine love, in the physical world. Wisdom insights to assist the conscious shift to light and love.
Anchoring the energies of divine love realised into the physical body, and hence our physical lives

Goddess of Destiny

I AM, Kwan Yin
Come to share my light of love
The peace of creation

I come to share
The mysticism of the divine
I come to share
The divinity that comes quietly

I come in peace
I come in love
I come shrouded in cloaks most divine
Yet invisible to the naked eye

Compassion overflows from me
Unending love from the core of my soul
A princess of peace
I AM, I AM, I AM

Creation is a mystery
To unfold quietly
Life is being – Love
Life is merging – Light

I AM, I AM, I AM
Kwan Yin
Goddess of Destiny

Leading with Love

What is the new frequency, which will lead us into heaven on earth? Love is that frequency, which is the true frequency and vibration of creation. Love is creation, creation is love. Creation without love is not possible – some strand of connection to the heart births this forth. Love is the chalice. Love is the womb. Love is the container of the frequencies of heaven. God is Love. Goddess is Love.

Conscious Feeling

Be conscious of what it is you are feeling. What you decide and choose to feel (yes, it is a choice!), will be what you eventually manifest. Even "reactions" to media news – it all GENERATES feelings, which shift your reality. Whatever you generate has to find a place to sit in your reality. Once you have generated that feeling – it needs a place to be, a place to rest, and eventually, if it is not something you like – it will need to be transformed and transmuted, or lived out somehow in your life. Either way, something has to happen to that energy. It will then need your attention to harn and synthesize it. It will not just evaporate and "go".

This was one of the failed key concepts learning that was not understood in Atlantis, and caused the sinking of the continent. Emotions were not readily understood, and the sheer POWER that love generates was misused – by splitting of the harmonic complete frequencies, in an attempt to understand their nature, and then duplicate and rearrange to be able to produce certain feelings at will, at times when they simply could not be produced/generated in one's life. This caused most of the sadness we see on the planet today, as the healing of this – to create a return to DIVINE LOVE is cleansing, and returning in healing harmony back to the whole. Subtle experimentation still goes on, if we "test" out anything in our living environment that has automatically been given in love, with love, by God/Goddess and the wonderful higher beings of light – and indeed your own higher self. It was approved at all levels down to the astral 4th Dimensional level. Low and behold – you questioned it at the last level possible – when it was just about to manifest! It is no wonder what some of you are feeling confounded and frustrated with life. If only you would know that this is what is occurring, you could get on with your lives by ALLOWING the flow. When something good begins to happen, do not question it. E.g. how long will it last? Is it too good to be true?

Allowing in Love

ALLOWING in Love is what allows your heart to flow with divine frequency, and the higher pulsations of divine energy. When you "play safe", withhold, withdraw, and do not allow the engagement of love into your life – then you shut out life as well as love, as the heart is the open hub of life in your body, which opens up and is a conduit for love emanation and expression of God/Goddess within you. This is why we feel more alive when we are in love. Do not fear what love can offer you. Do not fear rejection. Do not fear pain. Be love. Give love. Expand in love. As you let love in, allow for the overall picture of your frequency harmonic to shift. Do not expect to integrate it – and for things to be and feel the same. It may require the letting of the old, the situations and connections that did not work for you, or no longer work now. Make space for the new. Let go of distractions, let go of boredom. Let go of time-wasting. Believe life is not a rehearsal, and we are to be on stage NOW. Not later. We are not here to belittle ourselves, or play ourselves down. The objective of this life – is to expand in love, in magnificence, in glory of our God/Goddess spark within. The I AM THAT I AM.

Life gives to you on an "as needed" basis, according to your own commitment to your dreams. According to your own ability to conceptualise your new reality. According to your own ability to let go of the past. This includes letting go of old energies, patternings and ways. Every time we feel a different feeling, and GROUND this into our reality, it has an opportunity to create a small shift in your life overall, which will take you to a different platform of reality. Allow yourself to be fully present, and fully switched on, to the opportunity available in each day~

Open to Love

Open thy heart to receive the fullness of life and truth and co-creation with every other Being on line and in the moment, not withdrawing or pulling away from another while we check if we can trust that other...or to fear losing our self in the other...of losing our power, of losing our essence in unity. Do we fear we will not receive also, so we withhold, and monitor every exchange?

Do we seek to control what will happen when, yet sink into disappointment when we recreate each day the same as before? When we expect the typical of a particular day, and it arrives that way in accordance with our request, then why do we feel sad, disappointed, and miserable?

Why do we not open and take in life, so that we must continually repeat situations and actions, until we cover all levels of that which we were to receive? Why not receive all at once – if only we were open. We would never get bored. Never frustrated, for we would have allowed in all divine answers.

Do we need to analyse? Do we need to dissect? Rather to accept that which simply is, so we may take in all that it has to offer, as it is offered with the open heart? Is it not for God to oversee, and for us to live? Rather than oversee and try to live our life within that same breath. Once we try to oversee an entire situation, do we not remove our self from active engagement to our situation? Do you not think that other feels the removal of your consciousness to open active trust? Do you not think, as you withdraw your trust, that the other feels that removal, and that which was divinely planned and orchestrated, is unable to follow it's exact harmonic pathway, due to your lack of engagement to such? By the time you have analysed such – it has changed the dynamic.

Are we to be open in love, or limited by the restriction and lack of trust in unity?

THE KEYS OF THE FORCEFIELD OF LOVE NOW OPEN~~~

AS ABOVE, IN LOVE,
SO BELOW, LOVE OPENS IN FLOW
HEAVEN TO EARTH

Meditation

Be open to love, it may come in forms you do not expect...in the most unlikely places and ways~

Not all light workers have beacons!! Some do not even know they are this...

Open to loves flow.

To manifest – one must ascertain the specifics of what they need and why...and so shall it be...

E.g. If you are seeking a love relationship…maybe the core essence is that you wish for an everlasting love, and that is the divine core and signature.

EG.2. Maybe you want to teach groups, but the core learning – is to learn to handle the many different frequencies and messages of each person simultaneously…without going into overwhelm, and confusion, and then making sense of nothing…thus affecting your teaching and your own clarity and integrity.

Allowing

Expand INTO love. Allow love IN.

Allow that which you wish to manifest IN to your energy sphere. If you do not believe you deserve it, then it cannot come to your life. You must energetically allow it into your aura, and then integrate it – until you shift at a soul level. THEN and only then will it manifest in your outer life. It does this to MIRROR to you faithfully where you are at in your life.

Trust that only that which no longer serves you will leave you. That which is eternally good for you, will stay, and enrich your life, and expand your soul into a glorious magnificent expression of light and love.

Become transparent to negativity~

Responding to Life

How do you respond to life and people? Do you respond from a position of fear? Do you respond from a position of pain – expecting more pain, expecting loss?

When you respond from a healed and whole heart, there is no need to respond to another in such a way, for even in their fragmentation, you still feel your wholeness. Once this is filtered through, from the etherics (this change), you will experience more and more harmony in your life.

Aura Protection

Visualise Aqua/Turquoise, and opalescent light – around aura, with strips of white lightning of divine energy – around the aura – thick, like sheets of glass, to make the aura impenetrable.

Embodiment of divine

In order to embody the divine, sufficient integration of all of your life's events and lessons must be well within the physical fields of your aura, rather than floating in the other higher bodies. If the realisation has not reached the physical body, then the whole self does not shift, and manifestation is delayed by this. It could take literally years to fully awaken the body, if one does not realise this important step. It is also important to minimise drama and trauma, by living harmoniously by choice, and not reacting to everything that is put before you to learn by. Drama may be directed your way, but you are the composer of your own life, and can choose what instruments and sounds you have in your orchestra of life. Taking responsibility for this is what creates a shift, and brings spiritual maturity into fore.

Expansion of the self

Sometimes something that was valuable to you in a past life is no longer valuable to present life circumstances, but it is as though your value system is running on automatic pilot. For example – if you were a nun or a monk in a past life, then continued silence, poverty, chastity, obedience and aloneness, would have been very valuable for you and your life. Now translate that to a present life circumstance and you can see that you need to internally "transition" the value system to your new values. Somehow we think it happens automatically, but remember, the experiences are deeply imprinted and integrated unto your dear soul. What needs to be done is:-

Get in touch with an area of lack in your current lifetime. Determine this specifically.
Move into that energy space. Feel this fully within all your being.
Begin to see the pure pearl of wisdom that your soul wished to learn from that.
Begin to take the surplus energies that are not the core of your learning, into a violet flame spiral, transforming and transmuting to higher levels, so all that remains, are the lessons you were originally seeking. Anything additional will also remain, that is part of your soul learning, so do not worry over this.
Allow your entire system of energy bodies to begin to align, one by one. You do not necessarily need to focus or visualise, just feel them falling or clicking in to place, feel them mentally adjusting, emotionally adjusting and so forth. Until you feel whole again.
Enjoy the new found freedom!

Do not pull in the negative past into the present.

Forgiving and letting go – Do not hold resentments.

Allow your life to gestate perfectly~~~~

MORE REPATTERNING:-

1. Visualise a ruby cone – tiny rubies spinning down into the 8 original core points of the tail bone – repatterning your ancestry.

2. Now visualise a diamond infinity symbol – externally over the tailbone.

3. Allow the repatterning to enter into prismatic consciousness.

4. Visualise emeralds at your feet chakras.

5. Visualise sapphires in the pineal gland.

Divine Love Realised

Visualise white and God – and state:-

To you
I honour
With each breath I take
I love you
With every heart beat
You are my love

Opening~
To your soul…
In unity~
Magnitude
Radiating like a diamond
Sparkling through sun rays
Flowing on a summer breeze
Cascading like a waterfall
Soaring like the ocean
Silky like a barefoot beach walk

I am there for you
Embrace me
Engage me with your soul
For our immortal self is one
Sacred and Divine
Married in Love

Allow the sacred golden contracts to form and be sealed.
Forever
Amen

Meditation:-

Visualise your auric fields opening up like a rose – crystalline rose gold light sparkles upon each petal of your aura. Your merkabah begins to spin at high velocity – pastel blue, lemon, pink, and peach radiate and fill your being with the NEW light.

~Your life can be anything you want it to be~

The New children are coral in colour

The coral children are already unified, they know not of, or believe in separation...being aware of their multidimensional selves, and the cosmic field of oneness - they do not doubt that which they ask for is revealed, or even one step further of not needing to ask - knowing and trusting their own inner core strength always provides all, has the ability to connect with that which is in the unified field, and draw it into their "personal world". So to give a summary, they are self contained, yet inter-connected. They are love from a balanced perspective. There is no doubt. They believe and trust, because they know...no testing needed.

We are her in form only to materialize our souls dreaming – not to veer from this. Not to defer our path. Not to be deterred from the actualisation of our destiny.

Pure feminine. As a healing ray. Almost sweet violet sense. Prettiness, Charm.
Black Velvet Rose. Female depth and grounding within womanhood.
Peach/pink. Playful. Free. Creative. Fresh as the day.
Aqua. Deep. Contemplative with deep intuition. Self assured.

Overcoming

Complacency, Disinterest. Procrastination.
Drive – Will (power).
Energy for creativity. Timeless. Ageless (non-restriction).

~Remember – spirituality, love and light, come quietly~

First level – Love activation

When we reach beyond self-consciousness that restricts us, we can stay fully connected and centered within our soul, and let our light shine, like a diamond of the thousands suns – letting our multidimensional facets radiate through from galaxy upon galaxy.

Story of Love and Light (there is no separation)

˙ Let the universe connect and radiate through you.
The light

Vibration of Love

The "Right" Love is the only love. Conditional love is being a slave to love. How do we move out of the dramas of life? We allow for our spirit and higher self to raise our vibration out of the drama, therefore out of the continued calling to manifest drama. Allow yourself to rise out of the frequency band of vibration of the drama, the emotional, mental, spiritual and physical energies. Allow yourself to expand into the alternative that is ready for you, and believe there IS an alternative.

Flames of ignition – Chakra activation

Cleansing the flame rods within each chakra, to bring in the higher vibrational divine qualities

Choosing Love

I Love You
I knew exactly what this was
A moment of truth
An opening of heaven's heart flowed through me
There and then
Remembered in all ways
What could I do?
Knowing this moment was also for you
To share alike or give into fear and take flight?
Do we surrender? Or remain the greatest pretender
Ignoring the existence of this acceleration of our hearts
…but what our heart chooses seems beyond our own control
…yet why would we wish to control that which is divinely designed?
Why would we turn our back? On a gift fragranced with rose
Sweetly engaging our soul
Yet fear could disengage…
Oh this moment of truth is forever flowing
Our eternal moments of ~…all our lives~ Unfold with or without us
Cannot hold back destiny
Or the passage of time
But do we accept and receive this gift of the heart?

Acts of the heart qualities of the divine heart

Kindness, Compassion, Trust, Faith, Inspiration, Radiance, Bliss
Faithfulness, Loyalty, Devotion, Truth, Openness, Steadfastness
Forgiveness, Purity, Humility, Sincerity, Sovereignty, Integrity
Commitment, Clarity, Initiative, Generosity
Consistent surrender (to the divine)

Initiation into the new

I request the removal of all linear 3d structures that limit the expression of my soul, in its fullness, NOW.

I realise, that in order to function there in this world, that it is the NEW WORLD structures I must allow through from spirit, and allow that liquid light to form the new structures which support my unlimited expression of my spirit unto my fleshly body.

I TRUST spirit to support me as I realise the old structures of limitation, poverty, control, domination, and any modality or form that restricts the full anchorage of my soul in this lifetime.

I AM that I am.

That which I am, is a spirit of love, a spark of the divine, in flesh.

My boundaries, so to speak, are my unique divine mission unfolding and my commitment to this path unwaveringly.

Ask the light to go into all your matrices that are outdated and outmoded, that you took on for reasons of security and safety for your physical body.

House clearing/cleansing

Spin the Arc of the Covenant – in your house – to realign and reorientate earth axis in your home.

Visualise a rainbow arc above your house.

Allow in the christed white fire frequencies of light into your space. This is the new masculine light.

Sleepers of Civilisation
In Turkey: - Ephesus

In Egypt: - Great Pyramid Of Giza, Egypt.

Exercise:-

Merge with your sleeper.
The Rainbow sleepers – rainbow energy spirals through your body.
Emeralds and sapphires – midnight hue, enter the body and recalibrate it. Refashioning every part of you.

Exercise:-

Visualise: - Turquoise discs of repatterning move through the body, clearing all darkness. 144 crystals of counteracting divine merger (dualistic crystals) to be removed / moved from the crown chakra.

Meditation: - The chalice templates

Visualise a figure of infinity (8) with the lower loop circulating the lower chakras, and the top loop circulating the higher chakras. Within the centre is a circle or oval, in which the chalice template will anchor forth through.

Release:-
State: - I know willingly descend down into and embrace – all fragmented aspects of my being that need healing. I now embrace it all.

What IS your life pulse, which gives you passion, which makes you come alive?

The breath of life

This excitement I feel is the breath of God flowing in me
Growing in me, expanding my soul
To potentials as yet unknown

This breath loves me embraces me
Accepts me, caresses me
Loves we wildly, unrelentingly
For exactly who I AM

This one knows me, grows with me, loves me
Shows me how to live my life in the magnificence and glory
In the creators image

This one I love too
With my breath, with my body
With my heart, with my mind, with my soul

My body is his/her body
My soul is a spark borne of the divine
My breath is his/her breath
The glory is ours
Sharing in unity
The truth of the I AM (Love).

Do not try to do or be everything. We are all here in unity, to interconnect, to share the experience of life. We are a team of light.

Destiny search

Think kindly and gently unto yourself – what you wish to do with your life. Look to each element of that which you wish to become an incarnate expression of in your life.

Divine Tool

Using the harmony grid to bring into any situation, to harmonise it. Bring forth the grid into your situation in question.

Creative full potential

Clear all that stands in the way of the unfoldment minute-by-minute of in your life of tapping into your full creativity, and allowing for the understanding of how to utilise that as a flow, all of the time that you wish to work with this creativity birthing.

Secret of Life

Remain as the eye in the storm. Keep to your centre, the centre of gestation of the liquid god self within, the liquid gold manna of your I AM presence. In this cocooned centre for your soul, nothing can touch you, and you are the master of your creations, you are in power. That which comes to you, and you resonate with, is perfect for the manifestation of your own personal harmonic universe, and there are many harmonic universes that each person creates, and we get to choose to create our own, or co-create with another, or to enter another's universe to receive inspiration. We choose who and what we interact with. We can allow it to connect to us or not. The vibration will either lift and accelerate us, or slow us down and pull us down. We can remain in our own energy and choose not to respond to this drama. We do not have to engage in such activities out of "sympathy".

Acceptance of Almighty God Self

If you question your deserving, or all the good that you desire to manifest, do you not see that you also question God, or creation itself? There is no need to question. No need to analyse. No need to pull apart something to figure out how it is constructed. That construction is fluid and will always change.

Go forth and learn how to love without question, for this is the only way love can be love. Go forth and trust in the light, with your soul and spirit ignited within. How can you be the light if you do not trust, for light – is trust, and trust is light.

Speaking your truth

When you speak your truth, the creatorship rays go straight through to that person –

which then automatically received, as it is truth. It impacts, it unfolds. That person does not need to filter it, or try and discern the level of truth contained therein. It is direct, pure and simple. It touches, it opens.

In Closing

Closing invocation was created containing frequencies to move beyond fear, and in through the doorway of truly loving. All blame, resentment, bitterness, poverty, loneliness and all nature of lack of abundance is cleansed from one. It recalls, and yet moves through fear. In Essence, only love can move through anything, any darkness, any fear – right onward, and resume divine connection:-

Divine Love Realised!

Doorway of your heart

Can't close my heart
To the love I feel for you
When I run
Every-time I hide
It is right here
Waiting for me
To surrender
To what is

Open, beloved, the doorway of your heart
Let in the love
You seek to hide from
The love you ignited
From beyond time
Fear not
This love
Will not override
Your own self

I was honest, I was true
And in a moment caused you to feel blue
You closed your heart to protect yourself
But in love's truth
You cannot hide, you cannot run
It is right there
Waiting for you
To surrender
To what is
TRUE

As the works complete, Mary Magdalene enters offering a divine water cleansing. Open your being to allow for a full cleansing of all of your being. Take some time for the receiving of this final offering. Multiple stars enter your energy fields to clear all manipulation and domination from your aura. A white rose is given to you, to place in your aura. Star pathways open for you~

As time is an illusion, there is no such thing as time, if one projects ones desires and dreams into the future – then it is sending it away from you. Visualise it in this moment as being true, even if you cannot see it, you will begin to create it.

Opening the activation

The opening of the activation: - heart rays flood into the heart chakra front and back. Some extensive work will be done on the chakra, to cleanse all fear of opening to love. The back of the chakra will receive some extra love rays from the lady ascended masters. Christ droplets of light drip into the crown chakra of liquid light, to increase the higher self connection. Love droplets are placed inside the body cells, to raise the body to love frequency levels and cleanse away lower frequencies. The love temple enters from the multi-dimensions, spinning, and anchoring down to the earth plane.
The love temple is fuchsia/magenta in colour. The love temple opens up like a crystal lotus. We now enter the love temple, and each is given a gift of love. I was not told I need to know what that was – each person is to go into meditation to find this out. Once you have done that, you can come back to me, and I can explain it's purpose and meaning for you. The crown of life was given to us, and we become the living crown of life of spirit. Karma clearing takes place. We are given the choice to choose our life as it has been so far, or to take a leap and accept more fully our destiny book of life. The serpent of separation is released from our spine. The ring of love engaging ourselves begins. We are each given a ring of love, one of the love pink diamonds of the larger collective ring, is placed into our personal ring of love. Significant work takes place to cleanse duality and fear, any lack of love etc. Next the divine wedding takes place. Gold sparkling energy fills the space, as the divine wedding occurs. A yin/yang of gold sparkles spins – beneath our feet, bring us to a higher level of love, a profound love, a divine love realised. Each person received a garland of flowers – each person's flowers are different, this represents the peace following the activation of divine love. This was sealed with heart love. Finally, a deeply intensive activation of the subconscious mind occurs, a transmission of codes. This will assist in accessing multi dimensions, and making the unconscious self, more conscious. Your awareness will increase, of other dimensions and spaces. Allow this to unfold. Dearest light, may this bless you, and be gentle with yourself for 3 days following this, as integration will be slowly happening for you. Insights may unfold slowly or quickly, depending upon how much you are cleansing regarding protective amour around your body. This is something each person needed to release.

Divine Love Realised notes:-Clearing can be as simple as transmuting old impulses. These may have been passed on to you by another. If you can be transparently honest, then you can unify, for nothing will come between you and the other.

Removal of subconscious blocks - Sometimes the memory of a past life success can sabotage you, as if you do not allow the successful lifetime to integrate back into the melting pot of who you are in essence, it may also carry some karma from the experience. So instead, when recalling the memory – of experiencing a repeat of the success, you may experience your actions being constantly thwarted.

Divine Wedding

My Husband to be
I invite you into my life
To cherish our souls
May you grace my life
Embrace my life
…yours to mine…
….mine to yours…

For the first time
In rapture, in your embrace
For the first time
I am sure

The "Right" Love is the only love. Conditional love is being a slave to love. How do we move out of the dramas of life? We allow for our spirit and higher self to raise our vibration out of the drama, therefore out of the continued calling to manifest drama. Allow yourself to rise out of the frequency band of vibration of the drama, the emotional, mental, spiritual and physical energies. Allow yourself to expand into the alternative that is ready for you, and believe there IS an alternative.

Flames of ignition – Chakra activation. Cleansing the flame rods within each chakra, to bring in the higher vibrational divine qualities

The real thing is the intention first, and the action follows.

Chapter 7

The new love songs and invocations

Diamond of Love

A thousand years waiting for you
And one moment later you are there
Awakening my heart from its sleep
I feel alive, all my senses awakening

Shattering the ice that froze my soul
You bring me the sun that warms my being
Sounds of heaven run through my body
The sunshine finally arrived

I'd wandered so far, searching for you
I wondered and pondered where you were
How your life was~~~~~~~~~
Were you wondering too?

Each sleepless night I would reach for you
Awakening to a bed where you are not there
My tears ran dry from your absence
My heart made pale by your departure

My time for unity has come
Where every fragmented part is made whole
Where every dream is refreshed
Where every tear becomes a diamond of love

Love

Without love you're not living at all
It's the meaning of life
The heartbeat of existence
The essence of life
…being alive with love

Love…
Is the journey that we are all here for
It is the soul's reason for being
It expands,
It's majestic
Love is…the all

Seasons come, seasons go
The years in your life move on
Your life changes
…but…
Through it all
Is a thread of heaven
…in love

Cherished yet elusive for some…
The tenderness, the gentleness
Like a rose…of exquisite beauty
Fragrance of Eden
Does our heart unfold
…in love

The journey may be short, it may be long
Remain in love, you can't go wrong
Whispers of angels guide you along
Love will guide you to where you belong

We are One

To you~~~
No matter where you are
You are with me
Inside of me
Our souls as one
My twin, my life

The time is turning
Our time is near
To embrace as one
To reunite
To rekindle our love

My heart is alight for you
As yours is for me
An eternal flame
Of loving light
Radiates across the universes

The angels look on
As our time of union is here
Wise sages gather
To witness the blessed reunion
Of sacred love

Pure love, embracing
True love, enchanting
Sweet love, igniting
You and I
Forever, as One

Magical Love *Love Invocation*

A mystical figure in my dreams
Meeting my heart at night
Disappearing by day
…missing your touch

Weaving through etherical worlds
..Your spirit…I know
…our souls are as one
With your presence I grow

Be not only my mythical love
Appearing at dusk
Gone by the dawn
Knowing your spirit,
Yet not your flesh

Be my lover in life
My wedded one by day
Let our feet walk this pathway, as one
Our eyes gaze on this wondrous life

Let the dream come true
…yearning to be fulfilled
By the vessel of our love

Let your kiss release
All the past separation
Let the two rings seal our love, eternally

Includes coded energy keys to unlock various blocks to meeting the beloved twin
love/soul mate/twin flame.

Whole Heart

Picking up the pieces of my shattered heart
That came alive
From your smile
Years of separation finally come to a close

You are there
I have found you
Looking into your eyes
I know I found what I was searching for
I feel "home" in your eyes
The search is over
Finally~

Our joint memory
Our shared soul
Bares all
We wear our heart on our sleeve
Our sublime innocence
And our truth we do bear

Our smiles shatter the ice
Of the world
To run rivers of emotions
And deepest depths of the mind
Are open to the light

My Beloved

My dearest beloved
How I long to touch your face
Caress your loveliness
Hold you in my arms
Take refuge in your being
From the storms of life
Where every tear I shed
…a rainbow forms instead.
The flame in my heart you rekindled
Magnificent beyond all
Love is mighty, like the wonders of heaven
I'm cradled in your arms
I found a return to innocence

The One

That unbreakable bond
My one eternal
…flame
My beloved
Sacred love
…so divine
Sweet as heaven
Like nectar to my soul
Dewdrops glisten
In our field of love
Heaven scents linger
Of the union of our souls
The inner marriage externalised
A divine love realised

…in the flesh

New additions for 2010 Edition

Twin Merger

I AM you
You are ME
Twinned in destiny
Shaped in oneness
Unity is ours

You are I

You run with my breath
You merge with my tears
Not two souls, but one
A love beyond time
Love beyond fear
Always, in existence
Always, everywhere
You are I
I am you
One at last
Our eternal love
Bound eternally

Love invocation

Always knew,
I was waiting...for you
But time had not yet turned
To that moment
When stars collide
So our love could come to be

As that moment comes near,
I feel our love in my heart
I feel our union in my soul
I feel your breath in my breath
I feel your pulse through my veins
You are I, we are one, united
Our paths are merging
Our sparks of God
To meet in flesh

Merging

I want to merge with you
My beloved
My true (one)
My love for you is beyond this life
My feelings so true
For you, I wait
My heart, my breath
My soul breaths with your love
I feel you near me, I feel you breathe me
I feel you touch me, all around me
Exquisite heavenly sensation enfolds me
As you wrap your arms around me
I feel complete, I feel one
I feel you
My beloved
...I love you

Original Twin Flame

He is my blood, my breath, my all
So, why do I yearn that which I'm one with
Indeed also, why do we feel this towards God also?
When we already share the same breath
Two flames that are in essence one
Two hearts that beat in unity
Same smile, same touch
A mirror in the flesh

But, still I yearn you
To feel and hold you
To be one with you
Endlessly
A belonging incomparable
Indescribable
Desirable
To intertwine
Our love, our mind, body and soul
To rejoin
Reunite
To become that one flame we were originally
From which we did part
To become two flames
Endlessly seeking the other
Yet containing the other

Unity we all do seek
So deeply to our core
Invisible threads connect us
Draw us, mystically
To times, dates, events
That is alike
Until one day we do meet
In the flesh
In an ecstatic moment of bliss
And heartfelt remembrance
Do we finally reunite
…to become one

The voice of unity

With you, I'm the stars and the trees
A whirlwind in the universe
My heart alight with the pulse of the creator
Without you, my light dims
Sadness sets in
My heart swells with tears
To be one is the key to life
The breath and the mist
The inner bliss
....love brought me to my knees
A humble and noble beingness
Oneness - says the voice of unity.
To touch the earth
To touch the sky

Oneness
A Valentine to mother earth

The sweetness of the earth mother, Gaia
How I love thee
Your body of earth cradles my body and soul
From the depth of your waters
Oh holy mother of Gaia
To the heights of your mountains
You give us all
From the nectar of your foods
Nourishing our bodies, your children
Oh mother Gaia
You give us all
With beautiful animals to share
The beloved land that is you
The sacred land – our soul playground
You set the scene
That we may live a life
On your beloved soil
Sacred earth
Sacred Gaia
Love manifest

Quintessence of Love

Chapter 8

Quintessence of Love
The Unity Template

The quadrinity of life – opening to love

Sacred Hearts, I come unto thee, beloveds, upon this cherished day, I Mary Magdalene, ask you to also come with an open heart, unto the energies of this message, let the doorways to your soul open, so your spirit may take flight in your life, and your life become an elevated principle of love and light, let you become a masterful being, a being whose full capacity has become known.

How indeed does this happen, when you live your life running to and fro? When you struggle to embody a balance, and are always fretting and yet yearning for your dream? When you have no idea of how to balance body, mind and spirit, for you struggle so to realize how this may be done?

The essence dear ones, is to live the essence of spirit, by be-come-ing spirit ignited into thy body, oh ones. How I adore this opportunity to engage in such a message, along with the blessed beloved divine mother behind me, ushering my sharing, as I have awaited the divine timing for delivering such message unto you.

My heart sings to guide you upon the pathway of remembrance of true love, and to know this in all your relationships. To know how to live this. Do you know why my beloved divine counterpart Jesus, said, that you must become innocent as a child? It is to have a pure heart, an undivided heart, which resonates with the pure frequency and vibration of true love. This is for love, for the sake of love, rather than only romantic love, or those who may have been hurt that deliberately avoid romantic love. LOVE does not CHOOSE, Love simply is. To be LOVE.

Upon this auspicious divinely overlit day, the heavens open unto the truest of all loves, and the sacred Garden of Eden is thus healed of the long history of separation that was caused by knowing something other than good. This caused illness, aging, bitterness and much more – by the absence of love. The closing down of the heart chakra, to be selective over love did much damage, as the heart emits light, and so if it closes, the light cannot circulate, and what is left? Darkness – dark corners of your heart.

I will share with you, upon this day in February of 2009, some sacred secrets regarding the heart doorway, and will dispensate the sacred ceremony of love, that all innocence of light and love may be restored, and the inner sacred heart chamber will be imbued with energy of activation. The doorway of the heart will be fully opened and connected to the divine realms of source.

Until then, I wish you blessings and the love of my sacred heart,
Mary Magdalene.

Photo taken at Mont St.Michel, where this chapter was anchored on Valentine's Day in 2009.

Feeling the love

When you have not felt that love in situations: - with your parents, siblings, at work, or any other life situation, it often becomes to be something that you embody (you feel lack of love in your body) and this extends out to your world. The lack of the love rays in their fullness affects you, and how you act (with or without love), from love or from fear. With openness or restriction. In expecting respect or allowing yourself to be walked all over

The magic of love

Science attempts to separate in order to understand the magic of life. This is not possible, for there is magic in each union. The elements of each union cannot be duplicated to another union, and this will "click", for it is not necessarily so (not necessarily possible), and even if it does also fire sparks and unite, it will not necessarily be the same. This is the magic of love.

The focuses

As we prepare for the anchorage of Quintessence of Love. This is so you know what energies are currently running, and thus can take advantage of that flow - to open your awareness, and assist your own preparation.
Current focus that is running:-
Currently: - Clearing false unions that are not founded upon love.

Focuses right now on preparation

Clearing old modes of being - clearing "associations" for example...Sunday is a family day. and so forth...allowing freedom...of association to days or other aspects of life.

Healing the body back to the womb, where any restriction of love occurred during conception, gestation or birth - covering the entire time in the womb. Any time where you were denied or restricted the flow of love and light from mother / father God that you needed in order to grow in love, and have all the tools necessary for life on earth.

The Eternal Dream of the Soul

Which way round does creation work and thus manifest? Do you visualise and feel that which you love and your soul desires or do you go about a practical physical life, and tie it in with a written agenda of specifications?

Well, it all begins at the blueprint stage. It is orchestrated by your soul. Overlit by your spirit. And to be implemented by yourself that resides and lives in your body. However, bear in mind – only part of you lives in your body...the other is free as a bird, living multidimensionally, at that same time. To be free as a bird, IN the body, is the life you want to live. For your spirit to be the orchestrator of your life, for your soul to be the director, and your physical self to enjoy the grounding of the dream, by acting upon the messages – the instructions. Following through with what appears like ideas, like inspirations, to you. By making ROOM for this in your life. By ALLOWING it to be, by giving it time, space...by believing it can come true, all the way – and OPENING up to the universe to provide you with anything it materially requires. Life should not be measured by material, but it should work the other way – you decide what you need to live your soul dream, then OPEN and allow it to come to you, by magnetic of the universal law of "knock, and the door will be opened unto you". The door of the universe, that is. Then the final result is the dream clothed in matter – it has meaning, it has heart, it has soul in it. It is not empty or temporary, but an eternal dream of the soul.

I AM Omnipresent – an invocation to spirit of life, the soul of being

Across the doorways of time
I connect to mine own selves
Swirling through parallel doorways of lives
Back to the glorious past of my own magnificence
I retrieve all that is good and godly
I acknowledge my evolution, my growth

Sparkling, I now soar to the heavens
To visit my higher self
Angels surround me, playing their harp
Now memories of my original self
Flood my conscious mind

Feeling, deeply in my heart

I now travel inward to my god self within
I feel the heart of my soul
The depth of my being
Suddenly I know who I am, what I am here for

Glints of light come forward to me
Through the portals of the future
My future me! Encourages me
To complete all that she/he desires for me
Blessing me eternally by her/his vision

Created in rhythm to ride the waves of time, that allow for a smooth entrance to the passage of the truth of life.

YOU are the pathway

How many times do we look for an existing pathway in our life? Only prepared or courageous enough to tread the path that others have trod. BUT you are the pathway, that pathway is inside of you. As you move through life, you create a thread of life, which creates a new pathway: - the pathway of you. Your will and divine life pattern are the map, and your physical body moving throughout life in a manner that believes in your messages, create the thread of light REACHING the physical - by believing enough to act upon divine inspiration. Not following existing paths, but trusting in your unique invisible pathway - that only takes form once YOU act upon your messages within, with faith and courage. Way showers often beat paths that did not exist before. That is why we are the way showers. Because we have the courage and mighty divine fortitude to tread on pathways anew, and create something new for the world.

Tread on the pathway you desire, for that is the only way you are going to be on that path (get to that path)...You must BE that path...

Who you are

What you want and who you are, are intrinsically interwoven. Don't be afraid of the preparation to become who you are (and what you want)

Living our Dreams

How many times do we dream our dream, only to tell ourselves, it cannot be?
Thwarting our own chances of actualising (manifesting) our hearts dreaming in reality - to have in our life. Thwarting the enthusiasm of our inner child?

Mont St Michel

Light of the heart space

As we usher forth, dearly beloveds, upon this wondrous day of light magnificence, we take a step nearer to the light in the heavens, to ground this in its original light code signature, which you begin to learn to live and breathe love, as a natural process to your cells of the body. We will engage with each person present, a light signature that allows for pure love to be able to pass through the bodies codings, thus purifying the emotional elements with the body that have become engrossed in lower emotional interaction with life. This will allow for a releasing of all that is not love, from your life.

A pure light signature comes in upon us, preparing the way, to know of true love in all its forms. To distinguish this and to fully engage in a life filled with love. The pure love frequency is the most powerful of energy in existence, as it contains the frequencies, codings, light, sound and so much more, that is the true life. How many times have you felt that the life of absolute harmony is something outside of you, like you are looking through a window able to see all of the beautiful things, yet the window will not open, and the door near it is locked.

We bring unto you, the gifts of knowing the secrets of the heart. For those ready to engage and allow their heart to open to the deepest levels possible. The songs of the heavens (light) will ring through each level of your being, bringing a remembrance of the last time your heart was fully open and free of any emotional baggage.

Sealed in the divine white protective light of the heavens,

Namaste,

Archangel Michael

Lecture Notes from Workshop on the above channeled piece

This piece was channeled at Mont St Michel:-

Do you remember on the Gold Meditation you were given a gold signature? To place in the higher heart? This is the signature they are talking about. It contains the frequencies and codings that allow everything else to unlock. Also like a description of Plato's cave, that you are not opening to the fullness of life. We are working on these energies in order to feel everything. This will give you a feeling of desiring to unify with everything and everyone.

When you come into this world you have that vision of unity, and you want to unite with everything. Then you meet somebody, so then you close. Spirit tells you - not the one, not yet, and you explain to this one what you have been told.
So there is lots of unity, lots of connections, but it is the belonging, connecting with the true ones.

There is more peace than ever to always being prepared to move along onto what is next on your divine pathway, because you are always at the exact energy point that you need to be at any particular time (not holding back). Enjoy and thrive on the energies of transformation like a phoenix.

Discussion of qualities of love: - included seven/eight keys such as faith, knowing, trust.

Meditation at Mt St Michel in the Gardens

Allow the magnificent levels of light that is activated within this site and your own body, and you now visualise the core of Mont St Michel, a circular ring of light, spinning around anti-clockwise. This allows for a connection of all the ley-lines (earth grid/crystalline grid). Allowing for the earth shift that is necessary at this time. I would now like you to concentrate on your hara in your body (between the solar plexus and the heart). Archangel Michael now brings a swirl of light, from the centre of Mont St Michel, into your body - in an anti-clockwise movement, spiraling into the new chakra, releasing with it Aqua coloured light, representing our awakening from the subconscious sleep. The patterns of this that are programmed in your body, from the time of Atlantis, and the fall from grace, take a deep breath as you breathe in this light deep into the new chakra, and allow the spinning action to spin the aqua light through all of the pathways of your body. Release old harmful cords and connections, to places, people and things that are no longer part of the reality you are deciding to opt for right now. Increase the flow of this aqua liquid nectar, through every meridian in the body, and every etheric meridian which we call axiatonal lines. Take another deep breath in. Archangel Michael now brings a diamond into your third eye, spinning with light, allowing for a release of all suppressed pictures and experiences that are stored within the third eye, helping to free up this area of the third eye. He now gives you a beautiful diamond for your throat chakra, spinning very fast at the speed of light, clearing everything that you wished you had said - that you choked this in your throat (held back), and you did not express this. Lady Nada brings a beautiful crystalline rose colored heart, faceted to the most beautiful form ever. It glistens and glitters as she brings this near to your heart chakra. This heart is the secret essence of love, the forgotten essence of love, for the love that we have seen on the earth plane has been through so much distortion, until it is almost unrecognisable, and this is why so many people are confused by love. Breathe this crystalline heart deep into your heart chakra, and inside it opens up the altar of your heart.

Quintessence of love quotes

"We change our past by what we are doing right now".

"Just thinking and believing in something will help it materialise - to happen in your outer life".

Affirmation: - Only I have the map (of my destiny) inside of me. Follow the inner map first!

"The things you see in your future changes, when you change the path you are on" - in other words, life is flexible and changing all the time, according to your life choices, your decisions.

Current cleansing: - Clearing the 7 original cells at the base of the spine of the "serpentine matrix".

Thoughts to meditate upon: - "Where is your belonging? With whom and where".

Divine alignment - following on from the Da Vinci message in December, is to get out of the last grips of laziness or tiredness, so that you can move on and accomplish your destiny. (Sometimes it is actually ourselves holding us back due to fear - so it uses tiredness at times.).

Faith: - to receive manifestation of your dreams completed.

Physical: - Strengthen your soul through activity - by allowing your soul to be the one to choose the activities you participate in.

...It is all about the meaning of life, the soul behind everything. What drives you. Not about material possessions or even places, but the people you need to connect up with for your shared missions and events you need to be part of, to fulfill your destiny.

Quotes of love inspiration

Creation has got to come from fluid source energy flowing through you.

Prepare to fall in love with life.

Allow yourself to take in the greater life – absorb and become one with what you love in life (don't hold back, and/or wait for later).

What if....the reality you have seen all your life, is not the true one? What if the true life of love has yet to be discovered, and thus lived? What if....?

What is meant to be will always surround you.

The Beloved Twin – the other half of your soul

The Twin Fire
Burning higher
Breathless to the soul
Of the unification totality
The dance of unification
Echoes the past of separation

Yet by the love, the reunion is forged
Beyond times past
The life of the now
Is glowing
Awakening, unfolding
A vision shared, unique to us
To walk the path, as one
Seeing the same, being the same
As we are (so)
The trust is imminent
As one trusts one's own soul
Gently reaching out
That never failed to occur
At the time we requested, with all our heart
And a readiness of our soul
The destiny is unity, is sacred union of the lovers

Rose of Life

This rose of life
Carefully crafted with our attention
It does not just happen, but by our alignment to will
Each word
Each thought
Each vision
Then…reaching out, stepping out
TRUSTING, FAITH
Then what was invisible becomes apparent, our path is now before us
Ready to step upon
Glittering, glistening, encouraging, inviting
Never be afraid of set-backs, for we are at a time of great clearing:-
You only lose that which never belonged anyway
And retain unity with that which is love, and in love with you~
SO Cradle your rose of life, the rose of your heart
For you are dear to the divine, you are a beautiful flower in the bouquet of life!

What is love?

We are here to love, simply and purely. The only way this can happen, is to allow ourselves the delight of vulnerability through the opening of our heart fully. Anything less is not loving fully, anything less is a game at love, by putting up barriers that shut out another rather than protect us from being hurt. Those same barriers repel love from our life. The quality of love we can give and receive is not the same under such conditions. Love in its true nature is flowing; it is unconditional – only dependent upon the free flow of light from our heart chakra, as is flowing from our spirit, to our body. Our spirit never wants to have boundaries to love – only unity. Our soul does not want to experience withholding upon certain conditions before love has been "earnt" by another. Love of spirit just falls in love, or falls into unity, with those resonances that it is destined to be joined (unified) with. It does not know a time, or procedure, but it just wishes to express this flow of heart light, in the excitement of the reunion. It does not want to schedule a time when it is convenient to reunite, or "according to society" how long a reunion ought to take at each stage, each turn – the soul finds this tiring. The soul wishes to rejoice and allow itself to be overwhelmed with love, so that love is flowing, to the brim, and over, flowing through the chalice of the soul. For that love does nourish the soul and body. For dear ones, you have been so asleep, that often the body responses are the ones you may recognise, such as a more physical love, of appearance or animalistic urges of the body. BUT the heart seeks something less temporary. The heart likes the permanent soul love and recognition of the eternal flame of the heart.

Quintessence of Love workshop transcript

When we begin to open up the energies, it is going to go into a very deep level of your being; it is going to go right to the core of your being – the foundation of who you are. That will be the first thing that we will be doing. So it is basically any part of the foundation of who you are. So any part of the foundation of who you are that is not founded on your highest possible self that you could be, is going to be opened up for transformation. So my suggestion is to open up as completely as you can, because then you will have this wonderful transformation of your core self, your foundation to leave at the end of the workshop with. You'll have a big transformation. So, it will shift your personality and who you are on an axis, like a full 360 degrees, you will be in a different space of looking out, and responding to life and what you attract will be very different.

Any questions? Answer: - only that which is founded on any part of your personality that is holding you back. It is a good opportunity to go into this area and be prepared to be vulnerable and to change it. It is a very vulnerable space to go into a deep emotional space within you. It can make you feel vulnerable when you go to a very deep layer and level. Another example, perhaps you have old wounds, which are seated at a deep level, and you dig into that level to transform it. Then it is finished, and then you go onto the next level, you make a shift upwards, rather than repeating old ways of being. It is a very good idea to open up to this very deep level, and then it gives you the opportunity to make the maximum changes. In other words, the best way to do this, is to completely open up. Spirit have shown me how to work with this energy and the best way to make forward progress with this is to open up to the absolute deepest level of yourself emotionally, because then we make the shift onto higher levels of love inside our body, let the energies of transformation do their work. The deeper you allow yourself to open up, for the energies to come in, the more transformation that you will receive at the end of the workshop.

Spirit will bring through lots of support. So, if you have always wanted to make this leap into different levels of emotional experience, and not to be held back by older responses, emotionally this is the time to open up this level.

You are opening your being. It is like you have to open yourself up to the energies and spirit so that those energies can touch and go into this area. You open up your energy body so that they (spirit) can work on you. It is a good idea to open up emotionally. If you are trying do to this closed, how can the energies of transformation go inside and change anything? It can't because it is closed. So it is not going to quite work the same. Maybe it tries to come in, and you say – I'm not sure if I'm ready, so it goes.

Part 2

We bring forth the light, the keys of Isis, Mary Magdalene, Lady Nada, Jesus, El Moyra, Lord Kuthumi, The councils of light, The Nameless Ones from the central source of the throne of God of All that is, Aphrodite, the angels and archangels, to create a divine ring of space, of energy, within through and around each person's energy field within this group, individually and as a group, we create a golden globe of light around the entire energetic space, protecting and sealing ourselves in the light, only allowing that in which is for the highest good for transformation of the group, collectively and individually, that the highest codings and frequencies and vibrations to come from the spiritual realms, for the transformation process to be on a wave of love, easing any discord within the body, past, present and future. The light of spirit now ignites within each cell in the body, transforming all negative memory that is held within the body, which we will each move to a new platform of love.

We welcome you now to Quintessence of Love, We come on a wave of love – throughout time and space, from universes far away, yet we have known this one also. We enter through the gates of love, to bring to you a unique frequency, of love that is not known on this planet before, and you – each one of you – have volunteered to enter into this sacred space, of the flame of love, where you will work into and through this transformation, and come out the other side a changed person, where you can expect your responses to life, to be different than you have responded to before. This is a time, dear ones, to leave behind permanently, everything that ails you mentally, emotionally. How many times do you feel in your life something holding you back, of walking forward into the absolute greater expanse of who you are? Dear Ones, do you know who you are at this expanded level? And if not, we would like to introduce you to the greater part of who you are, that you will come to know, through all the transformation that is being offered to each one of you.

We now bring forth the golden codings of liquid light. Visualise this swirling into the centre space of this group. There will be a fork of golden liquid light fork out to each person here. Dear ones bring this into your higher heart, your thymus chakra, and into your solar plexus, now anchor this inside, and you do this by bringing the liquid light – into the centre of the two chakras I have just mentioned, directly through the chakra and out of the back, covering all time and space, past, present and future. Feel this anchor in, Isis now breathes in emerald energy over the front of your aura, and then this breath of emerald energy, like sparkling diamonds – glisten. You feel these diamonds awakening all of your forgotten heart energies. These diamonds of light, dear ones, are totally unified, they know of no separation. They are the perfect light and the perfect love expression, which is now being introduced into your form, your body. Allow yourself to be touched by this unique light. Breathe these beautiful glistening diamonds into your body, into your cells. Allow yourself to feel and receive a change in your emotional body. And, dear ones, fear not this change, for this is the next change we are all scheduled for, and when I say scheduled, I mean that those that are preparing the way, in other words the way showers (like you are shining the light of other people – you are a path cutter), for those that are in this position, this is your next step. Without holding these higher levels of light and love, we cannot expand to the next level of mastery. First you must gain mastery over your emotional body, otherwise you will sway and be buffeted around by life, and you will not reach your destination, which is your destiny. Take another deep breath in. Isis now seals this energy with a key of life over your front chakras.

We now open up this space, to the highest Elohim angels. They now connect through the centre of this space, their unique codings of mastery. They allow us to have an insight and sharing of their highest levels of pure love. Unconditional and a flame of love that burns like no other. A flame of love that is not afraid, ever, to burn in its brilliance of love. Those with psychic sight will see this flame from a very long distance away, because the love is burning so bright, through its purity, through its trust, and it is these qualities that we wish for you to step into. For this is a mastery that will transform and change our life. Take another deep breath. And now you will see within the centre of this space, a pool of water – glistening – beautiful. It is full of angelic codings, to allow you to wash away any experiences in your life, that are less than you would like. Please dear ones, now observe your reactions to this pool. Do you dip your toe in, or do you dive right in? What are your emotional reactions? Feel this beautiful glistening water around your body. Allow anything that is troubling you in your life, which you wish for a total recalibration of, to now begin to melt away into this pool. Submerge your head into this water. As you move inside this water, you will notice a very deep level of clearing taking place, a dissolving of old hardened patterns, begins to occur. Take another deep breath. You will notice in the centre of the bottom of this pool, a spiraling staircase, going into another pool underneath. This staircase is made of crystalline energy. As you begin to descend this next staircase, you feel your vibration shift and change, you almost feel an excitement within the body, as it activates deep memories, of everything that you hold on a subconscious level, which you have closed away and shut off, out of fear. As you descend this staircase of crystalline energy, you see beautiful dolphins swimming. You feel their energy support you greatly. You feel them looking at you – calling you, communicating with you. You feel a stream of energy coming from the dolphin, and it moves inside your heart chakra. You feel a piercing feeling as this enters in, for the reason that their energy is very pure. Their love knows no fear. Their love simply IS love. They now bring forth a healing and a recalibration. We feel this beginning a restructuring of your heart chakra. You now feel old pain and hurt that you have still stored within your heart chakra, times when you have opened and you have been hurt by another. You feel a very deep healing from the energy that the dolphin is giving unto your heart chakra.

Their pure light opens new doorways and new levels. Levels you have even forgotten yourself, because you shut them away too long ago. Dear ones you know at this level that you have closed off to, this level also contains the capacity to hold joy. When you close off for fear of pain, you also close off a segment of your heart, from experiencing and receiving love, joy, harmony and beauty, your heart's desire, the living of your dreams, your ability to accomplish your destiny, because your heart is a navigation system for you, through feeling your heart, you navigate your way into your destiny pathway. Your heart flame lights the way forward. This is your map. This is how you know that which is right for you for this life. This is how you know what you need to accomplish on a soul level, to learn the soul lessons. Ones that benefit your soul and spirit. You now ascend the staircase, thanking the dolphins as you rise. You now move into the first pool, feeling a very different person. Feeling a higher level of opening, in the heart chakra because of the dolphin frequencies. And as you move into the first pool of light, now begin to release off of your energy field, energy blocks, old stagnant energy, that is no longer for your highest good, to remain anywhere in your energy field. This part of the energy process is now sealed in the light, by the angelic councils of love, and they offer each one of us here this pattern to hold. You will see a white scroll that is unrolled in front of you that shows you this pattern. Hold this pattern into your heart chakra now. Absorb this pattern. Feel the frequency of this in your heart chakra. Feel now the level that you will be opening up to over this weekend. Take a deep breath.

MEDITATION – ENERGY WORK

I want each one of you now to think and feel of your hearts deepest wish, for that which you would like to touch upon this weekend. What is the most important thing for you right now, as a soul - to transform to, emotionally, with your heart - as you move into love...? What do you wish to leave behind you? What baggage do you wish to drop off now? What do you permanently say goodbye to? What part of your reactions as a being on a human level do you wish were different? Take a moment now to set the intent, and define what is important to you. As you think of this hold this desire, this deep wish, into the flame inside your heart. Now take one moment to do this. Take a deep breath as you do this. For each person, who is wishing this weekend to receive a particular transformation into higher levels of grounding the divine, to bring in new qualities, to your human self, you may now request the frequency that begins the process, of a full transformation to your higher levels. Take a deep breath as you now allow this frequency to connect into your heart chakra. For those that have very big wishes for the transformation, we feel some of you present there that have some very big desires and wishes for the transformation this weekend. I ask for you to request now more than one special high frequency. If you have a very big mission that you are working on and you find that you are struggling to keep up with this mission, this vision, if you feel the dreams of your soul are far, far bigger than your human self is moving in to, I suggest to you, I recommend to you open up to a multitude of frequencies now. If you feel a very big gap between your physical self and your spiritual self, open up to twelve frequencies, or if your mission (and gap) is bigger, twenty-four, or thirty-six and so forth. Of course if your mission is very, very big, or you feel the gap is way too big for you to reach, call in one hundred and forty-four threads of golden light. Whatever the number you have chosen, feel these special threads of light now begin to plug into your heart chakra. If you have put up many barriers of protection for your heart in the past, you may feel a tiny pain as the cords of support go inside your heart chakra. In which case just relax the heart chakra, and know that all is well. Breathe this directly into the heart chakra - into the middle, and to the back of the chakra. The frequencies, sounds and codes of heaven now begin to anchor into the heart chakra. Take another deep breath. Very, very slowly begin to come back into the body, bringing with you all the magnificent frequencies that you have experienced, firmly into the physical body. Please take a couple of moments before you open your eyes. Re-orientate yourself back into the physical body. Stretch your arms and legs. Take another deep breath as you allow the energies to firmly seal into your body, bring yourself back very gradually.

SHORT MEDITATION ~ ACTIVATION

Take a deep breath in. We now bring unto you the purest light from the highest levels of divine love; we bring this into the solar plexus, allowing you to feel the energies of the power of love. Allow this energy of love to saturate this chakra. As you absorb one lot of this energy, you call forth the next lot of energy of this light into your chakra, so as you absorb one lot, you ask for another until you are full of this energy. Now, look inside of this chakra of solar fire, look inside at the patternings in this chakra. Does this chakra look strong to you, or weak? Take a deep look. Feel the energies inside this chakra. You may find that you are drawn to one pocket of energy in the solar plexus chakra. Allow yourself to gravitate towards this energy. Now, feel the frequency. Allow yourself to see a picture of when the time when this energy implanted in your chakra. When did you store this energy? What situation caused you to suppress this energy? What test of power have you not passed yet? Now take a moment to allow yourself to travel inside of this energy, to learn what you need to do to empower yourself, to discover that which you need to transcend. You may see several pictures or something like a video playing, of the situation that you need to transform, before you can come into your own personal power, allowing you to fully step into your mastery, and to be ready to step into the energies, that we will transmit tomorrow. This very short meditation will kick start the energies and these energies will run overnight, swirling and merging in your dream state, allowing yourself to move into the space where you can be 100% tomorrow for the energy work we will do at Mont St Michel. Please take this opportunity to leave behind all emotional baggage; do you really need these bags anymore? No, they hold you back. It is the time to know who you are, that you may step into the portals of your destiny, and to have the tools that you need, to find this pathway, and to keep to this pathway. Not to stray, not to be afraid of stepping onto this pathway, to have the inner clarity to know which is the pathway. Take a deep breath now.

PYRAMID MEDITATION

In the centre of the room you see a beautiful pyramid. From the outside of this pyramid, you see a beautiful colour that is a blend of lemon, silver and gold. It is glistening, radiating the absolute light of the new universes. The light is so bright and brilliant; it almost takes your breath away. This pyramid is spinning clockwise, representing the ability to take you forward into the future, so you may gain a greater understanding of yourself. I'd like each one of you now, to stand fully in your being. I'd like for you to encapsulate who you think you are at this moment in time, and do not move forward until you have encapsulated this into words. When you are ready, you'll see a ring in this room, outside of the pyramid, and when you have encapsulated the essence of who you are right now, a symbol will appear on this ring. When you see this symbol, step into the ring, and you take a leap into this spinning pyramid. As you do so you will feel your energy accelerate vastly. You feel yourself spinning forward. We ask you now to move quickly into the centre of the pyramid, where it is still. It is like the eye of the storm, and this is something you each need to master, of not being controlled by time. We have something to teach you on this. It is an illusionary veil. Underneath your feet you will see lots of numbers, like they have fallen off the face of a clock. This represents you moving outside of time. You will see yourself sinking into a seat in the centre, where you are to contemplate who you are outside of time and space. When you lose the restrictions of who you are by definition, of linear three dimensional life, but who are you as a soul when you release definition of your job, your living location, your standard of living, what you like to eat, what music you like, who are your family for this life, friends, relatives, ancestry, places you like to travel, need we go on? For the moment let all of this drop. Come into the centre of your personal eye of the storm. Who is your soul? All these things we mentioned before - we cannot be defined by. Give yourself a moment or two to feel this definition.

Night Time Resolution

You each need to call forth a resolution in your night time. You are each given a pattern of light, like a circle of filigree metal. It is like a personal key to prepare you for what is next. Place this in-between your thymus chakra and your heart chakra. Pat it into place with your physical hand, with your right hand. During your sleep state, before you ask for the awareness of what this key means, allow it to take you where you need to tonight, and know that great light and love will follow you, throughout your dream state, and we will be ready to greet you in love and light tomorrow. May you have beautiful, swift transformation, with absolute ease, grace and beauty. May your soul flower, allowing the most beautiful expression of your spirit to anchor in this lifetime. Now we bring this to a close. Put your hands in prayer position over your heart chakra, as you now come out of the spinning pyramid and back in your body, a beautiful turquoise light surrounds your body, sealing in all the energy work that we have done tonight. Namaste. Very slowly come back into the body. Stretch your body. Take one more minute before your open your eyes.

Notes:- You can expect some deep transformation overnight, in the solar plexus. You might find psychic cords begin to dislodge from this area - and come out. You will feel a greater sense of wholeness will come to you. Tonight you will have a process of repairing anytime that you felt powerless. So, I suggest as you are falling asleep, you affirm and allow yourself to go into a very deep level with coming back more fully into your power.

Mont St Michel Abbey Activation

Greetings dear ones, we welcome you unto this sacred space that you have waited many lifetimes to return to, where we open all of the doorways of light, and the difference is on this occasion we are going to create a divine balance between the masculine and the feminine, a transformation for the planet earth, Gaia. The light overcomes all darkness. I invite each one of you now to feel the energetic transmission coming into your soul, focus on anchoring these energies into your soul, and your soul is going to become like the disc of ying and yang, that it is totally balancing into white light, that contains all of the colours of the rainbow.
A physical activation took place at the Abbey with Crystals.

A crystal circle was set up in the center of the Abbey and then:-

I would like everybody to center and feel grounded here, keep the spine straight, take a deep breath, as we are doing the earthing.

Energy work took place afterwards.

A crystal circle was set up in the center of the Abbey and then:-

I would like everybody to center and feel grounded here, keep the spine straight, take a deep breath, as we are doing the earthing.

Energy work took place afterwards.

Now centre the energy in the centre of the space where we are, and all the energy that was built up by workshop participants sending back and forth to each other was spiraled down into the earth (you may picture this also). Now you visualise mother Gaia receiving this, opening up, and she sends this spiral right up through the centre of Mont St Michel, and it spirals up through the etheric pathways right up to spirit.

Thought to meditate on: - do you have any issues of the heart that are not healed?

ACTIVATION OF THE FLAME OF THE HEART (meditation)

This big flame in the heart is now large enough to burn the pathway in from the heart to the higher heart (from the heart chakra to the thymus). Once this pathway has opened through the burning of the energies of divine love, and light, the secret path of unity is now opened, never to be closed again. You will be carriers and way showers of the true love frequency and you will each individually and collectively notice a transformation in your personal life, and every person whose lives you touch by your presence. Take another deep breath in now. You now notice some sparks of the flame that is now touching the thymus higher heart now enter into pineal and pituitary gland in the brain, sparking the connection of the mind to the heart. Allow these sparks to burn away lower mental debris. You feel the energies of transformation in the mind, and you now notice a glow of violet energy around your entire brain area. From the sacred temples of divine love, they now weave into the centre of your brain, a golden white spiral of light, connecting through all of the glands in the brain and in the body, firing up the entire energetic system, moving and overriding all mechanisms of separation - whatever form the separation takes, it is now your time and your place to heal this completely. Whatever elements of darkness you have ever known in this or any other life, you may now release these. And now we complete with allowing Archangel Michael to clear all cords that are not of true love and not of the true belonging - to be cut/severed with the sword of light. And we now call in all connections of our destiny, our soul family, our twin flames - our love connections, to merge with you, so - in your body where there was no love, there is now love, and unification. Now visualise a figure of infinity in front of your body to seal this meditation. Namaste, we are done. Slowly come back into your body and your awareness (physical) and open your eyes when you are ready.

ALIGNMENT FOLLOWING MONT ST MICHEL VISIT

I would first like to begin by taking you through an alignment, of the work that we have completed at Mont St Michel, to integrate everything in its proper place, so that you may feel and benefit from the entire activation, in the form that it was intended, as channeled by spirit. If you would like to close your eyes, if you have not done so already, take a deep breath, allow yourself to center in your body, and now feel yourself arrive etherically at Mont St Michel. You are now standing in front of Mont St Michel. You don't see yourself small in comparison to Mont St Michel, you see yourself more connected energetically rather than in relation to the size of Mont St Michel, do not concentrate on this part of it. You are now going to see yourself on an iridescent, opalescent platform that is spinning. This is at the energetic gateway and opening of Mont St Michel. You feel a bubbling, sparkling vibration at the bottom of the souls of your feet, as you begin to open up to the portals of love of the earth. Your body somehow receives a message that is now to open up to new levels of love, and let go of everything that has previously been experienced that is not of love. You begin to see your body as though through an x-ray - you can see directly through the body. You can now see clearly any areas of darkness. Just take a moment to feel these places, to locate them. Take a deep breath as you do. Archangel Michael now brings a sword of light through your spinal column, as this moves through the spine, it cuts all the linear pathways, removing all illusion and veils, because, dear ones, it is for you to know that love is truth, truth is love. So, whilst there is any illusion, or pretence, or exaggeration, or anything that is not of the absolute pure truth, how can this possibly be love? So we are here to show you love = truth = light. You may use this in any combination, for all elements are interconnected, but alas, so far, this is not how the world has run. Do you know why? Because people are fearful of love. They fear the vulnerability. They fear the exposure of their original innocence, for fear that they will not feel their power, but there is the power of love, of spirit and light. Spirit now brings a spiral through the crown chakra, a spiral of light that is beautiful, pink, opalescent light. Allow this beautiful light of love to dissolve every single encapsulated stored thought that is in your mind, your brain, your mental body, that holds you in denial of love and this also includes anything that you have seen externally in your life, when you have experienced another person acting in this way. We can tell you, dear ones, there is no need to identify with this. For in the identification of this, you take a moment to step out of love, as you focus and concentrate on the lack of love, in an attempt to understand it, you move out of the flow of love, and once the flow of love is broken, you are indeed vulnerable, and this is the only time you are vulnerable. Whilst you stay in love, you are not vulnerable, for you are connected and unified, with everything that is love. The essence of life itself is love, so you cannot be not supported. It is not possible to feel unsupported, even when you are in an experience when your love is not returned, dear ones, do not take this to heart, literally speaking, for you are always receiving love from the universe, from the source of all that is, from the angels, and everyone on the earth with an awakened heart. Just know now, dear ones, these ones that cause you to feel that your love is not being responded to, are learning and resisting the lessons of opening their heart to a new flowering of love. You now notice a beautiful portal open that encompasses the entire Mont St Michel. You feel it as a liquid energy of light. You notice a pathway of crystalline steps, open up and moving into the centre of Mont St Michel. You suddenly feel eagerness in your heart and a memory through all time and space, that you were destined to do this activation. As a group, we all move onto the steps on the pathway, into the centre of Mont St Michel. You now notice a spinning action occur as you move to the centre of Mont St Michel. A powerful surge of energy vibrates through all of your energy bodies and all of your chakras. It dislodges anything that you have been unable to clear so far. Everything can release if you do not hold on to the identifications of the pain. You have the chance to move on to a new way of being: - free of pain. Allow this vibration to loosen up every single area of your body, where the energy is stuck. We will give you a couple of moments to do this. If you have any areas that are stuck and you have trouble dislodging them, you call upon a beautiful being of light, Archangel Michael, into the area of where the problem exists. Allow it to beam into the problem areas, giving light unto the area of darkness. Allow the light to illuminate the true meaning of the situation you are holding onto. Allow yourself to let go of the situation and trust in God, to do the transformation for you.

Let go and surrender. The guardians of love of the temple in the higher realms, now bring through the most beautiful templates, new templates of love: - free of fear and duality. The templates are of the most beautiful patternings as you look at them. You bring these fully into the body. Infuse one into each chakra. Take a deep breath as they seal into your body. Feel the patterning unfold from the template. Feel the new level of love open within the chakra. Lodge the template deeper and deeper into the chakra. Allow the light of the new patterning begin to shine out of this chakra. The Elohim and Lady Nada now bring forth two diamond crystals. One goes into each side of the temples of your mind/head. As it moves inside of your mind, it spirals around as though it is a ying/yang symbol. As it does so, you feel a relaxing of the mind. As all mental concerns and thoughts begin to erase and clear from your being. El Moyra now brings forth a beautiful faceted diamond of many, many facets - into the centre of your brain. It illuminates the conscious and the subconscious - every area, bringing a new strength, light and power to the mind, allowing for a release of duality. This light now moves through the entire neural pathways. Allowing for a release of all tensions, all contractions of energy, every part of you that has ever resisted life. Allow this clearing that we have done so far to move through the entire body, until everything has cleared out that is not of the highest good. You now see a disc in the center of the brain, which is made up of many segments of sapphire and emerald. You feel the strong vibration of the sapphire and emerald, connecting to the key part of your mind. You feel the essence of truth of life; open up in your mind, shedding a new light on your thoughts, feelings and reactions to life.

Strands of light now come from the disc and wrap around the brain area, and plug into various parts of the neural pathways, causing a new firing of the synaptic pathways. This allows a new connection between the conscious and the subconscious. A new balancing is felt now, from the mind to the heart, as we have been building a new strength of love in the mind, and a new feeling of destiny, of direction, within the heart. So that the heart knows the highest qualities of the mind and vice versa. Thus the pathways between the two strengthen, instead of working in opposition with each other.

You marry these two parts of your being. You now see another spinning disc, behind Mont St Michel, behind the entrance (on the opposite side). This disc is black and glittering, representing the void of life; allow all discordant energies that are left within your body to drain out through this disc, and into the void of life for a repatterning and transformation. Feel the gravity beneath the disc begin to pull all energy from your body that you no longer desire to remain with you. Take a couple of moments to do this thoroughly. Take a deep breath, release as much as you are able at this time. Including allowing for the release of any pattern or situation in your life that is not according to your truest joy. Allow for its release and its repatterning. Give yourself permission to change that which you do not like in your life.

FLAME OF LOVE

You now see a shower/rain of light coming down from the heavens, droplets of clear nectar, allow this to be absorbed into your body, cleansing away any last debris that remains from this clearing. If you feel there is alot to clear, accelerate the absorption of the rain. This beautiful nectar rain is offering you a return to the original innocence of love, where the conception of anything in your mind or heart that is not of love, is not possible. or the purity and the exact patterning's of this original love is held whole within the heart of God and has been since the beginning of time and will be until the end of time, at the birth of new worlds to come. This pure heart flame is held within the center of all creation protected by many multitude rays of light, to hold this in its exact original intended form, to hold the integrity of the love, for anyone who wishes to return to a state of pure love, may do this at any time. The flame of love will never leave creation. It is the flame of love that begun all creation. It is the originator of all of life, birthed from the flame. You now visualise yourself coming back from the staircase, the stairway, a beautiful blue light surrounds you as you move to the entrance, and you find yourself on a crystalline platform. Use this place to shake off any last debris. All thought forms and feelings may be dislodged now. All fear, all doubt, can be removed at this point. As this crystalline platform connects with the original crystalline body within your being, you feel a strengthening of your aura and your ability to release and shake off that which you do not desire. The crystalline energy from the disc moves up and connects firmly with your crystalline body, strengthening all of your etheric pathways.

BAPTISM OF LIGHT

We now move through another pathway of light, opening up in Galilee, in Israel, where we are invited by Jesus, to receive a rebirthing. He now ushers you forward, his eyes full of love, this arms open. You feel the truth of the essence of the heart radiate from his being. He welcomes you into his arms, and you surrender to his touch of love. Take a deep breath, as you let go of all the troubles of this life, and all lives. He strokes your hair back, and you feel the comfort of his sublime wisdom. It touches your heart, touches your soul, allowing for a greater strengthening within you. We take another deep breath now. He invites you to receive a divine baptism within the waters that surround you now, allowing for a further ignition of light and further purification within your being. If you feel ready allow yourself to submerge into the water, supported by his arms, as you do so, you feel the cool of the water, and the strength of the arms of Jesus holding you. You begin to feel the surrender into love, on a greater, deeper expanded level of your being. All petty worries now begin to disappear from your being. Enjoy being bathed in these sublime waters. Feel the sacredness within your entire body, reminding you that you are birthed from God, and you have the spark of God right within the core of your being. You are divine. You now emerge from the water, and you gaze into Jesus' eyes and he gazes into your eyes. He looks into the core of your soul, and when you look into his eyes, you feel the reflection of your potential. All your reactions and your resistance to life, all these begin to seem unimportant when you feel his divine strength, his divine majesty, and how he carries his mission within the entire essence of his heart. You feel him enraptured within his gentleness. You feel in awe of his strength. The many qualities within one being, inspiring you to create the same within your own being. He gives you a ring to seal the baptism, of one simple diamond solitaire - reminding you of the wholeness of who you are. Although you are united, you are also whole as an individual. This is the gift of this passage away from unity (talking here in reference to the original passage away from source). But we are now on the pathway back. For everything that belongs will be unified, and everything has a belonging, so everything will be in its perfect place, order and form. The new order will form. You feel immense joy in your heart and mind as you rise from the waters, you feel and see the vision within you of the plan of Jesus' lifetime, the purpose of his mission, and everything regarding his life. He touches your head.

You notice on your head you wore a crown of thorns. The pain of feeling the separation, reminds you of any part of your body that holds any sadness within you. The tears of the angels touch the crown of thorns, and you notice the entire crown becomes glittering crystalline. It transforms into the most beautiful crown. And you suddenly realise that the pain was just an illusion, which we never needed to believe in it, and buy into it. That we are pure beings of light and love, and we are just here to be that and to radiate the light and love. You feel a relief as you realise that is all you are here to be.

Pressure releases from the mind at this point, you feel relief in your entire body, you realise your soul purpose is to move into your entire embodiment and divinity, and to anchor this physically. Jesus now gives you a beautiful blood red cloak to go round your being. Sealing you in the protection of the real bloodline of the sangreal. You see two chalices swirling in front of you, as we complete this meditation. You are seated in the most exquisite chair, as you now feel an anchoring of everything that we have moved through in this meditation. This chair spirals anticlockwise, and you feel yourself now spiraling back into your body.

QUINTESSENCE OF LOVE ATTUNEMENT

Allow your heart chakra to open, to allow for the frequencies of quintessence of love to come through as an attunement, and an infusion, allow this to open the heart chakra front and back, clearing out every frequency in this chakra that is not of pure love. Allow old pictures of old situations to now begin to release from your energy field. Lady Nada now comes in front of you, she touches your crown chakra, and as she does so, all the blocks between your physical bodies and your spiritual bodies begin to melt. There is a crystal behind your eyes, which holds the illusion of separation in place in your body; she now removes this for you. Take a deep breath as this is pulled out of your energy field. Jesus comes forth now, carrying a beautiful crystal of unity that he places where the previous crystal was. You feel a cool feeling of peace. The peace of the dove, of the Shekinah. Lady Nada now removes a crystal that is between the higher heart and the throat chakra. This has been preventing the energy from the higher heart flowing into the throat chakra, so that you can speak of love, and speak with love. Take a deep breath as this is now removed. Jesus replaces this now with an emerald crystal. Lady Nada now removes a crystal that is in the left brain lobe and one in the right lobe of the brain. This gives the illusion of duality. Take a deep breath as these are removed. The Elohim angels now replace these crystals with beautiful brilliant diamonds that are of the most unusual nature, they contain gold coloured codings, to allow your mind, to join with the mind of God, which knows everything is unity. Lady Nada now moves to the back of your energy field. She removes a crystal that is in your 7th cervical, which is where your neck meets your back. Take a deep breath as this moves out of your energy field, and Jesus comes to the left side of your energy field, at the back, Mary Magdalene comes to your right hand side. They weave a web of love around your energy fields, allowing you to feel cocooned by love, on a physical level, so your body feels the comfort and nourishment of this divine love on a physical level. Please keep legs, arms/hands uncrossed during this process. Jesus brings forth a crystal that is the colour of sapphire and aqua blended. Mary Magdalene now comes forth, with a crystal that is the colour of fuchsia and rose. We now see the two crystals join together, and they are placed within the 7th cervical. A thread of spiral light moves from each crystal spiraling down the spinal column, activating Jacob's ladder within your energy field, your divine pathway up to spirit, and your own pathway to connect all levels of your being. All pathways of separation - at this moment - collapse within the energy field. The sapphire/aqua and rose/fuchsia radiate through your entire aura, healing every time you have stepped away from love, every time you felt fear, instead of feeling love. Know this is how much love you allow yourself in your life. You are the commander of your life; you can choose one of pure love.

To be compromised by nothing. Take another deep breath as we prepare to have all crystals within the shoulder area that block the back of the heart chakra pathway to be removed. The higher surgeons of light now come in for each person present here; they remove every further area of blockage from your energy field. Everything that you are waiting to release at this time. Everything that has limited your energy body, to one that feels something less than divine, everything that limits your divine gifts from unfolding on a physical level, to be cleansed from you at this time. We now move into the flow of the Quintessence of love ~ flowing through our being ~ into our soul, allowing for a higher coding of love to anchor through each being present here, through all time and space, all levels of our being, multidimensionally. Everything that is not at this level of love can now be dropped from your life. Permit yourself the release of this now. As you continue to allow your vessel to be filled up with the Quintessence of Love, a beautiful lemon, rose, white and gold colour emits from the soul of your being now. A deep healing of transformation now occurs at this time. You see the fires and the flames of transformation and transmutation burn away all density from your body. Inside your being, you see one singular rose, which is a beautiful mid pink colour. The fragrance of the rose enchants you, beckoning you into further depths of love. The flower reflects and heals through every cell of your body. A ring of white roses now spirals around your aura, bringing you a return to innocence of love, to a space where you have known no hurt, no harm. Refreshing you from the long journey of your soul, breathe this new energy in. Allow, again, to release everything from your aura that is of a denser nature.

Take another deep breath. Jesus now brings you a golden rose. Cup your hands to receive this. You will see inside the petals of the rose - platinum codings, of the highest, fastest frequency. As you look at these codings, you will see that they will move into your aura, merging with your being. You will see, feel and here messages that are of pure love, that simply do not know the absence of love. Take another breath, as you place this rose between your heart chakra and your higher heart. Take a very deep breath as you allow this to expand into the core of your being. The councils of love come into our space now, bringing forth a bundle of scrolls, come and take your scroll from this bundle, and return to your space - and unfold this scroll, which will light up as you do so. You feel an energy so ancient, so present moment, and so much of the future also. This scroll seems to contain the ability to emanate of all times and spaces. You realise it is your scroll of love, your plan of love for this lifetime, and every lifetime. Allow yourself to take in the magnificence of love that you are to ground in this life, because as you ground this in your life, this touches every life, past, present and future. You will feel the codings within the scroll move very fast. The immensity of the light and the love, almost takes your breath away. For they are the beautiful codings, to merge with your soul. Allow all contracts that you have ever made that do not fit in with this beautiful reality to be cancelled - if you are ready for this deeper level of love and life. If you are ready to ground this, and have this realised, in physicality. If you wish to live this and see this in manifestation, cancel everything that is in opposition to this now, by your intent. Take a deep breath as everything that is not love begins to release from your energy field now. Every time you have felt separation, release all of this from your energy field now, and the causes of this, release this also. We are each given a beautiful cloak of love, lemon/white and gold in colour. You are invited up to the higher realms, for the blessing of love. As you ascend the most beautiful ornate staircase, you notice a rose colour all around you. A beautiful crystalline landing is before you, and you feel most magnificent, pure and radiant as you step on this platform. You are greeted and welcomed by Mary Magdalene and Jesus, who hold up a chalice of love. A droplet from this chalice falls into your crown chakra, dissolving all pathways of separation.

Jesus requests you open and place the right palm of your hand in front, a cross of light and a heart of light is now written on your hand by Jesus. Mary Magdalene places your left hand over your right hand, and places a bracelet with a rose droplet on your left wrist. As you place both hands together, you feel the pure energy of love union - of sacred union. For those who are ready to manifest their sacred union in their life, please place your hands over your heart chakra now. Allow that energy to enter in to your heart chakra, and that if you choose to request to manifest the sacred union on an external level, in this lifetime you may choose this now.

Monaco – Adam & Eve
Divine Love Realised

Chapter 9

SPECIAL ADDITION: - *This special addition was anchored at the site chosen by spirit – just under one year later from the original distance workshop. The energies complete the work of that year, and also of the twin love energies in their collective form. It is now time to manifest the divine compliment, our divine counterpart, and live this love. Be with this love.*

Meditation: - Divine Love Realised - Monaco Meditation in the Exotic Garden

Dearly Beloveds we open today, on the breath of love and the breath of life, the chance to open new doorways and new portals that allow you to experience the essence of love and light in their perfected form upon the earth. And we close now the portals of abuse and misuse of power, where the energies of creation have been manipulated and distorted, until they end up taking on a grotesque form. Take a deep breath now beloveds, as you breath in the true breath of life, one that is free of hatred, free of distortions, free of chaos, free of doubt, that you may begin to know, learn and live life in the fullest. Now beloved ones visualise three pink flames of varying depths of saturation of colour, within this garden. This garden holds these energies perfectly from its original form, ancient form, and current form, which now blossoms in beauty of a natural form. Take a deep breath now as you breathe out every memory and judgment of the love of power, for dear ones everything must be in balance, and the love of power alone was already lived at the time of Atlantis, but hence beloved ones not all of these learnt the lessons of the flow of life, for the love of power requires one to store and hoard, maybe suspicious of life and also on the same score – everything becomes conditional – the flow of life is broken, and everything requires and needs to be healed all of a sudden. To heal is simply to reconnect the flow of life, which is present naturally. To be conditional interrupts this flow. People are not as clever as they think when they hold back things, whether this is be love, be money or any other element or expression of life. Take a deep breath now and take this opportunity to release out any past lives or any times in this present life when you have felt the need to be conditional. These flames in the garden grow brighter. Around the edges of these flames are beautiful silver and platinum sparkles of light. From these sparkles of light, move lines of light that move up into the heavens, these create a time line of healing, making a further clearing of the separation of life. The turning of one's back on God. Take another deep breath as you release this also. A beautiful tree of life moves from the bottom of these three pink flames and touches the earth. Feel this connection into the earth of this original body of light, the tree of life. Adam and Eve stand either side, but not in their separated form. They are wearing golden cloaks of light. Adam places his hand on eve's heart, and eve places her hand on Adam's heart. A beautiful flow of forgiveness and reunion begins to flow. Reconnection to Unity. And you feel now from the ancestral tree from which you are also born. You feel their reunion heal you also, you see inside your body now, a duplication of this pink tree of life. You feel a deep healing in the body, a return to love. Adam and Eve stand either side of your body, and as they touch your shoulders and the back of your heart chakra, you feel a deep healing of all hurts that you have experienced in this life and any other life, including all parallel lives and lives off of this planet, and also including spaces between lives when you are waiting to incarnate again, and this includes all types of incarnation, whether a human or a dolphin, whichever body you chose to come in, angelic, Egyptian – whichever your choice was. A beautiful golden spiral now comes through your crown chakra, Eve places her hand on your crown chakra, you feel her deep love for you and her love for humanity in general, and your whole body melts under her love. This loves fills you, it does not leave parts of you yearning to be quenched with the love, for this is the original love; this has ignited the eve body of light. You may have heard of the Adam kadmon body of light. This is the eve body of light. Allow your heart to heal any fragmentation that is still there and present. Feel a deep healing and coming together of all shattered pieces of your heart. As this happens, you notice a platinum flame on the edge of these pink three flames in this space. You now see a crystalline staircase. As you enter this staircase your whole vibration in your body changes. You feel true love as it is felt from an angelic level, and you feel this throughout your entire body. You allow this to flow through all of your chakras, allowing this liquid light to heal you, soothe you, and calm you. This energy feels like an embrace of your being. You are having the opportunity to embrace yourself in the love and light of all that is, by knowing and feeling and being this vibration of love. And feeling this as it is stepped down from spirit and into your body. These beautiful angels are on the staircase as you look to your left and your right, and you look into their eyes and you just melt into the love of all that they are. And you know that they are love and nothing but love. There is not one bit of darkness in their eyes. And the look in their eyes encourages you to let go of any parts of your shadow side. The look in their eyes encourages you to not be ashamed of any part of darkness you still hold. They now wrap you in the most luminescent beautiful cloak you have ever seen in your life. You feel wanted and welcomed in your life like never before. You feel a rebirth. Allow all distortion, chaos, anything within your body – all negativities – now to just release like a flow of water through you. They placed a beautiful crown or tiara on your head, representing your alignment to divine levels. You notice rainbow colours radiating through your body right now, consuming and transmuting all darkness. Take a deep breath now, as we move down a staircase that is coming down to the opposite side. And each step on that staircase brings you slowly and slowly back into the physical body, where you once again embrace the life that you are in this lifetime. Namaste. Take another deep breath and continue to release out everything that no longer serves you. Slowly open your eyes when you are ready.

The original audio meditation recorded live in Monaco is also available direct at www.lulu.com. Search under author name: - Sarah Ince.

Divine Roses

The red rose
Is before you
Of a love so true
It is eternal

One your heart could not forget
Despite the years
Of "moving on"

A white teardrop glistens
With the centre of the rose
Promising peace
With surrender to this love

A black glistening teardrop
Is within the folds of the petals of the rose
Allowing an entrance to the deep healing
Of your heart

Blue Christ light surrounds this wonderful rose
Magenta light glows from the petals core
Inside your heart
You feel a deep synthesis
Of the very fiber of your soul

All at once, you remember your pathway
Look before you now
Dear one
It is golden with platinum sparkles of light
A sense of peace is restored within your being
This peace is sealed within you now

Photo taken in the exotic garden in Monaco.

ANSWERING READERS QUESTIONS:-

Yes, if someone meets there twin flame, it is possible, also to meet their twin ray here on earth - providing they have the desire for this, and is part of their destiny. Twin love assists you to key into the different resonances through the exercises - to help those who wish to manifest those connections. Regarding the different levels of reunification, imagine a vast sea of love, encompassing many different levels of love, from the most subtle and exquisite in its expression, through to different levels that one may possibly be "working at" or surrendering to - in order to fully acknowledge the divine love that one is. As you begin this process of inner unification, you will reach more refined energy - as you move through any blocks to accepting and being total pure love. This will externalise as "reversing" the journey back through various soul bonds that you formed on your original descent into matter and through the illusion of separation of the veils. The levels discovered so far have been outlined in Twin love, including Twin Spirit - as the fourth level that was channelled in Cyprus. Since we were originally birthed from source, there were many splits/separations that created all the different levels of soul love / twin love and soul families. Regarding the difference between the Twin Flame, Ray or any other level, is by the purity of the elemental essence of such. The more one can embrace more love that brings unity - the closer one moves to experiencing greater and greater love unions - or reunions with those who we experienced the different levels of split/separation - so in effect - we are moving through, and reversing the separation, as we reunite, and heal the pathways - more of the same may occur, until we are face to face with our beloved only one moment before a unification occurs - for we are one, and it is evident. The love expression at this level is the most refined and subtle - a gentle love that knows or needs no questions, no demonstrations, it simply IS.

AFTERWORD

Each level of Twin Love workshop has taken me on a special journey, both inner and outer. Following the workshop on Valentine's Day 2003, I met my Twin Flame about one to two months from this time. We met through the music project I was working on at that time. We ventured forth to the Island of Iona for our second meeting where we were to fully acknowledge our connection. Past lifetimes as a nun and monk surfaced up, and was quite challenging at that time! And of course it may indeed feel like that – as we prepare to open ourselves up to the deep connection that is to be shared. Each person present felt propelled on a mission, and some of the workshop participants were assisted personally by my cupid self. Later that year, another level of Twinship was birthing forth: - The Twin Ray. Little did I know this would have me trekking over the ancient sites of the land of Turkey! Initially guided to visit the site of Troy, this trip triggered two later return visits (all in 2004) – to connect with significant members of my soul family, and of course to include my Twin Ray Love. Healing and opening as I traveled from Istanbul to Troy, and then onwards to Cesme, Izmir and Kusadasi, each trip opened the doors of my heart wide, as Turkey is literally live with the expression of the open heart. Karsiyaka was my final destination, on my final return trip, where the most significant healing of the love fibres of my being occurred. At the same time, I assisted one of the people on the course, as she felt guided to meet her beloved also, and received great healing from this connection. The Sacred Union Cd was recorded following this time, with the energy inspirations from Sacred India. I met my last significant connection to date whilst receiving Sannayas at the most beautiful meditation resort in Sacred India in 2005. Destiny somehow aligned the peoples to receive Sannayas, which I was to receive Sannayas at the same time as this special love connection. I made many friends who no doubt were soul connections steeped in past life history. I kept in touch on arrival home with some that I met in India. I also met a new friend from my home town that was from India, which helped me on other levels, complete this connection. The journey is one of true love, of opening to deeper and increasing levels of love and connection. It is always about rising in love, never about falling in love. Also the wider and deeper we clear emotional baggage from our being – the more space there is within for a pure, expansive uplifting version of love to reside – impacting all of our love relationships – including soul family. Love is opening up every part of our selves, being prepared to be vulnerable – allowing all doors to be opened by the key of love.

Allow all the preparations within this book to assist you to clear your emotional body and expand your heart. If you have not met your twin love, this may assist you to be ready for this event to occur in your life. The highest levels of love are beginning at this time to anchor on the earth. Many are not used to such high frequencies, and it certainly entails allow old pains to fade and heal – knowing there is a reason for everything. Something is healing or aligning you deeper to the highest expression levels of your spirit, within your life. For the higher love to enter, and the higher frequencies the higher love reside at, it requires a very clear platform – where it may house itself.

From a return to innocence, do we return to a pure state and sense of love. From this level of relationship, unity is possible – and then ALL things are possible, for we live from love, which is, living from the God and Goddess flame within. Wishing you the dreaming of your heart, that may lead the way to your love so true. It is with utmost peace of my journey of love, that I add the new updates in this edition. When you see in the other, your own self in completeness, you feel you have come home, you transform. Alchemical transformation, and energy information exchange leads you into completeness.

This level of love is all. It is the one from whom we separated originally – as we were held in the arms of God. It is called Quintessence of Love

2010 note: - As I update this edition, we move nearer to Valentine's Day of 2010. I have met so many people that worry to take a step into commitment for fear that their freedom will be taken away from them. Commitment is only an affirmation of the existing love between two people. If you have truly met your match – your true beloved – there will be no sacrifice, as you will be on the same pathway, looking in the same direction. You will complement each other. This may, however, involve a shedding of that which you may be living out, but may not be – in essence – who you really are. This may include old habits – which you believe is who you are. Another point to mention here is that one needs to be fully open to love. This may not be as easy as you may think. Trust is important and remaining open. A lot of people fear…they fear if the other person does not call them back when they wish for this and many similar scenarios. Perhaps the other person needs some space to return to their own essence, as they work through their old habits that do not reflect who they truly are. Maybe this appears initially as unloving. Without such reflection – a pure "flush" connection is not made. It does not fit. This is a paradox, but one that must be worked through, to reach the ecstasy of true love.

On a physical level, it assists if one is in good health. I have been guided to alter my diet to an even healthier one (previously vegetarian bordering on vegan – with all organic produce where possible). The new diet includes juicing – freshly squeezed juice, fresh salads (part "raw food" diet at present), cleansing baths. This is opening up my cells and body to receive more life force – which, of course, includes more love – in a general sense – to include from source, to include soul family, our beloved, and all of life. It is the time to release karmic relationships that are based on conditional agreements. I was given an opportunity towards the end of last year to clear this more, and see more openly what this represented. When a situation that was similar to this followed – I was able to avert this – and there was no need to live this any further.

When we reach this point – we are able to stay in a state of openness, because we have learnt to say no, by recognizing that which is karmic – and releasing it for what it is – a conditional condition. Then, we are able to move on to total openness, and enjoy the journey to our beloved twin of the highest – where a meeting is a fusion of the divine masculine and feminine embodied, to experience that flame once more, on earth.

Namaste. Enjoy your journey to love.

We are the guardians of the earth and the caretakers of our body temple

UPDATE: - When we perfect our own balance of who we are and what we have lived so far (this life and past lives); we are then ready to merge and join with our beloved. If we do this too early, and we are not prepared, we will not have the balance within to bring to the relationship the best fruits of love, and thus the union will not be at its best. You will know the time for the union. You may feel hesitation if the time is not right, and on a deep level, be working at whatever is necessary to make this possible, as I have done myself. It involves perfecting oneself in preparation that you may be able to stabilise the fierce lively burning flame of love, that it may be eternal and never burn out. This Valentine's Day 2010, I finally perfected that flame, and my perfected energy was then able to merge with my beloved. How did I arrive at this? Working through many lessons, many life circumstances, some "good", and some not…but it was my reaction to all circumstance that counted, to remain balanced, yet remain in my truth – which is a delicate balance. When you achieve the balance, then you may approach your beloved and reunite: - the sacred union. I'm so happy this completed on Valentine's Day. Transcribing The Activation of the flame of the heart, and describing to myself who I really am on earth, encapsulating that, assisted the process. In coming into the truth of who you are, it is then possible to merge with your beloved twin love. You are then finally free to work as a couple on your life ahead, once you have defined your own mission adequately, and perhaps grounded that upon the earth plane through some physical action. Depending upon your joint mission – will vary the degree to which you need to have completed any of your mission separately. That is personal and individual.

ABOUT SARAH

Sarah began meditating at the age of 14. A decade later, her conscious path opened up at deeper levels, as she began an in-depth study, that later would lead her to receive divine visions and projects over-lit and requested by the divine to assist humanity. Sarah has been a channel for divine dispensations since 1995, although her first public offering was 3 years from the time of her first vision. Sarah is dedicated to opening up her own soul to her highest potential, and the wisdom she channels assists others to do the same. Sarah recently completed a series of workshops in France (translated into French), and has previously taught and led Sacred Site Journeys worldwide. Sarah is currently preparing a book series to include all of the teachings from 2002 to 2009, ready for worldwide release (publication).

Sarah Ince first began to write poetry at the age of fourteen, weaving the vivid expressions of the artistic scenery of the rural town where she was born. It would not be until her thirtieth year that she recommenced writing poetry, covering her spiritual experiences and expressions of love. Sarah's work has been published online in various magazines and ezines, including the Cosmic Lighthouse, Mused Magazine – Winter 2009 issue (Bella Online), Planet Lightworker, Your Spiritual Revolution (YSR), Sage of Consciousness (photography of Sarah and a musical commissioned piece according to her vision) – current 2010 edition, Paradigm Shift Magazine and many more sources. Also her poetry is published online where various poems of love are showcased at Harusami.com, and as part of the I AM Family Gathering website that was held in 2006. Her work also appears in "A passion for poetry" - an Anthology published in 2002.

"I usher in higher blueprints and visions through the dimensions, and work with energy to send them and weave the higher dreams into spaces where they are needed. I hold a higher frequency and vision within my own energy field on an ongoing basis. The unknowing might call this hope, but it is knowing that holding a higher blueprint and vision, brings the frequencies of this to imbue those sacred vibrations to bring into manifestation the creation of a higher birthing. Without the higher vision – the ability to hold this vision, along with the ability to conceive of this vision, there is no positive potential for change and transformation. One needs to be able to create a sacred space on earth – and this space begins to gestate firstly in the spirit, and then to anchor within the soul body – thus then transferred to the physical body through the blueprints, which are picked up and conceived in the mind. We receive this as impulses, if we are not a clear channel, or are distracted, which feel as an intuition. THIS is our opportunity to then implement this in our lives, and be able to live the sacred space on the physical – in the same high space as we created it through our visions (on the etheric).

I personally work with blueprints, which I have created 44 written ones, with meditations (audio and some written, others being transcribed) and with sound healing. The format has been for ascension, so thus describes what one needs to know for this".

ADDITIONAL TITLES BY SARAH INCE

You may also enjoy several related products by Ascension Light productions:-

UNIQUE SOUND HEALING CD's by Sarah

Sacred Union Cd: - Divine Language of Love mantras to open the heart and heal the emotional body.
Twin Spirit Initiation Cd – recorded in Cyprus.

Also available: - Cd: - Immersion.

These can be purchased at www.cdbaby.com and various other internet sources.

Listen to the sound healing online at: - www.myspace.com/soundhealing

Please contact author at the email address below.
For further details please write to the address at the front of this book.

BOOKS

ILLUMINATION - The complete works from 2002 to 2008
Available as EBook/Paperback or Hardback. Ascension Lightbody Paradigms to anchor the Golden Age upon earth.

www.lulu.com

Poetry and Invocations of light healing
Available as EBook/Paperback or Hardback

DIVINE TWIN meditations – available currently as MP3 downloads, and by request as CD's. Meditations recorded at the live workshop of Divine Twin.

INNER WEDDING OF MASCULINE AND FEMININE – is available as MP3 Download and upon request, as a CD.

The audio of Divine Love Realised is available as an MP3 download.

Monaco Meditation – Adam and Eve meditation of healing the Twin Split. Available also as an MP3 (transcript appears within this book).

Also available, the original love glyphs (oracle cards). 12 coded images for healing the Twin Love separation.

PRODUCTS: - Greetings cards, note cards, posters and much more – of the Twin Love Image (and others), may be purchased online (and customised) at:-

http://www.zazzle.co.uk/leiamera*

Sarah Ince, The author, may be contacted at the following email address:-

Sarahince1@aol.com

Website: - http://www.ascensionstargate.webs.com

You may join the mailing list to receive all future updates of new books, new editions, new cds and upcoming workshop events and excursions.

Stargate Alignment
A cosmic rebirthing event

Greetings Beloved Ones,
At this time of great change, the shifts are felt deep within, rocking many to their core:
- this core is only what has been known to them so far, consciously, about themselves.
It is time to rock through the core, breaking through the old encrusted matter that
defined who one is, to learn of the pure flow of spirit that resides within, that waits for
the freedom and limitless life – that waits to know the true life of light and love. Many
components and energies are currently gathering together, and a significant process of
"sorting" is coming – for the wise, who will sift out that which prevents their own
divine inner alignment, therefore their alignment with the life of ALL THAT IS.
Through this special alignment of energies, you will be prepared as a way shower for
the GRAND ALIGNMENT OF 2012. Make no mistake, this alignment that is
forthcoming – is an alignment of dynamism, of pure cosmic force aligned with the
heart of mother Gaia, for the rebirth of earth as we have known it. She is due to enter
her new age, as a new earth, as the embodiment and sacred matter of a living
organism, a living being that holds those who hold a candle to the truth, who allow
their inner light to be lit. The time for procrastination is over. You will be rocked to
the core of your inner light by the truth of your own soul, pulling up into the light all
that you have resisted, pushed away – until you cradle your dearly beloved self in the
heart of your own light, your higher self, and love that self fully into the light. Thus,
dear ones, this is an event of transformation, rebirth, of finally relinquishing the old. A
deep alignment of new cosmic energies that will provide you with the opportunity to
move from lost to found. The unique synchronisation of codings will allow for a
revealing of your true self, to allow the path of uncovering your dearly beloved soul –
to be less than troublesome, but a heartfelt joy. The frequencies coming through will
cover various lineages – so that all that accept the invitation to this weekend of
discovery – will have the opportunity to highlight, ignite and retrieve further
information on their cosmic lineage.
We, from the central source of all that is, welcome you with an open heart and
showering of blessings, May the true light dawn upon each day, Blessings unto you,

THE STARGATE PLAN

PREPARATION FOR 2012

Stargate preparation phase 1:- Beyond Definition – shining your soul light.

Without attachment to any previous soul definition – we come into a new light – our
soul's light, and we allow our soul's light to take the lead, leaving behind past life
definition and attachment to any previous identity we have held. We are rebirthed, we
are beyond where we have birthed from, where we have lived (this planet and others),
beyond the beyond: - we are shifting into higher frequencies, riding the light waves of
a new world, a new consciousness. Unless we take this opportunity, we will feel like
we are not moving, with the sameness of the old repeating again and again.

all comes from the same, ~~God~~ that is which
we call LOVE.

From a return to innocence we then return to
a pure state of and sense of love.

May I wish everyone our new song baby
and thank him for his message, his very being
showing us the return to innocence

A number of years ago The Saint Anendamaynan came to me in a vision, she give me a golden key: as she smiled at me a profound sense of love was felt

That Golden Key the perfect fit to unlock the door of the Heart.

On turning that Key, that day, my world has been spun around, turned upside down, tossed and turned ~~rock~~ to I've have been rocked to the very core of my being,

That Golden Key, that ~~released~~ on turning brought all of the pain, the hurt, the suffering, that I had ~~ever~~ ~~felt~~ been locked away from long ago times.

(Until I finally fall down to my knees and cry)

(I Surrender, I surrender

which has finally been brought to surface spilling over, spewing up, I fall, to the surrender, I surrender, I fight no more, I forgive.

I call upon the Elders, I sit in council with the Elders they tell me that the seal has been broken and the new door is now open.

A lightness is felt now as I rise, slowly and vulnerably, very fragile, but feeling much much love in my heart, in my very being

So, at this special time of year, known as the birth of Christ, may the Christ light be with you All, and whatever place of being you find yourself in, whether, pain, hurt, suffering, happiness, joy, laughter, ~~it~~ Always know that it